U.S.A. Wynn Bullock

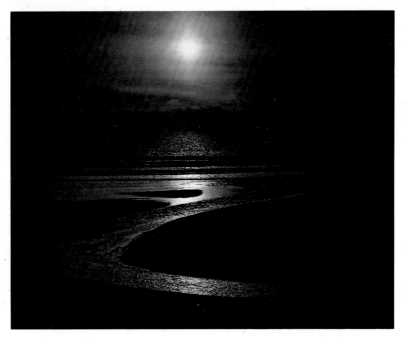

*And God said, let there be light*    Genesis 1:3

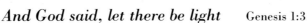

# The Family of Man

*The 30th Anniversary Edition of the classic book of photography*

*created by Edward Steichen for The Museum of Modern Art, New York*

*Prologue by Carl Sandburg*

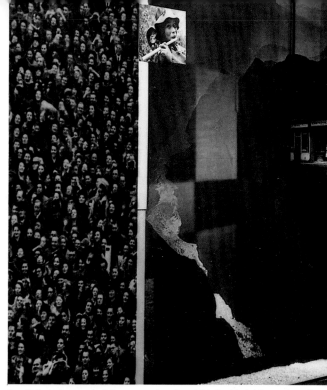

Ezra Stoller's photograph of the entrance into the exhibit. Paul Rudolph was the architect.

*Library of Congress Catalog Card Number 55-11621*

*Art Director: Leo Lionni. Art Assistant: Francis Gruse*
*Captions: Dorothy Norman. Assistant to Edward Steichen: Wayne Miller*

*Theme photograph of Piper by Eugene Harris, "Popular Photography"*

*Published by The Museum of Modern Art, New York*
*11 West 53 Street, New York, New York 10019*

*Distributed by Simon & Schuster, Inc., New York*

*Touchstone is a registered trademark*
*of Simon & Schuster, Inc.*

*Printed in Japan*
*ISBN 0-671-55411-5 paper; ISBN 0-671-55412-3 cloth/Simon and Schuster*
*ISBN 0-87070-341-2 paper; ISBN 0-87070-342-0 cloth/MoMA*

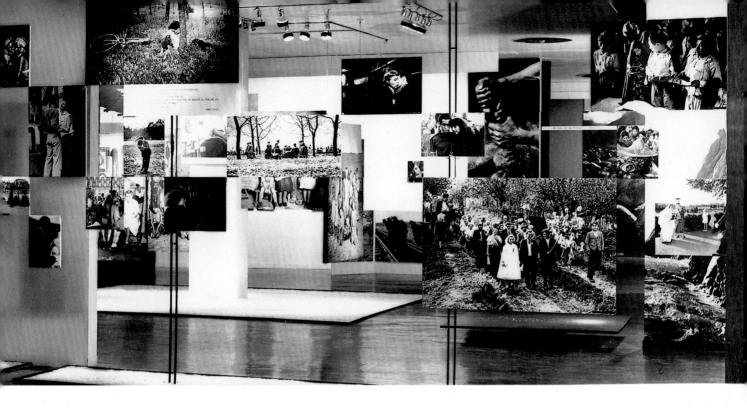

## Introduction by Edward Steichen

I believe The Family of Man exhibition, produced and shown first at The Museum of Modern Art in New York and now being circulated throughout the world, is the most ambitious and challenging project photography has ever attempted.

The exhibition, now permanently presented on the pages of this book, demonstrates that the art of photography is a dynamic process of giving form to ideas and of explaining man to man. It was conceived as a mirror of the universal elements and emotions in the everydayness of life—as a mirror of the essential oneness of mankind throughout the world.

We sought and selected photographs, made in all parts of the world, of the gamut of life from birth to death with emphasis on the daily relationships of man to himself, to his family, to the community and to the world we live in—subject matter ranging from babies to philosophers, from the kindergarten to the university, from primitive peoples to the Councils of the United Nations. Photographs of lovers and marriage and child-bearing, of the family unit with its joys, trials and tribulations, its deep-rooted devotions and its antagonisms. Photographs of the home in all its warmth and magnificence, its heartaches and exaltations. Photographs of the individual and the family unit in its reactions to the beginnings of life and continuing on through death and burial. Photographs concerned with man in relation to his environment, to the beauty and richness of the earth he has inherited and what he has done with this inheritance, the good and the great things, the stupid and the destructive things. Photographs concerned with the religious rather than religions. With basic human consciousness rather than social consciousness. Photographs concerned with man's dreams and aspirations and photographs of the flaming creative forces of love and truth and the corrosive evil inherent in the lie.

For almost three years we have been searching for these images. Over two million photographs from every corner of the earth have come to us—from individuals, collections and files. We screened them until we had ten thousand. Then came the almost unbearable task of reducing these to 503 photographs from 68 countries. The photographers who took them—273 men and women—are amateurs and professionals, famed and unknown.

All of this could not have been accomplished without the dedicated efforts of my assistant, Wayne Miller, and the tireless devotion of our staff.

The Family of Man has been created in a passionate spirit of devoted love and faith in man.

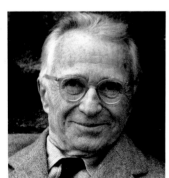

Caroline Hammarskiold

*Edward Steichen*

*Prologue by Carl Sandburg*

The first cry of a newborn baby in Chicago or Zamboango, in Amsterdam or Rangoon, has the same pitch and key, each saying, "I am! I have come through! I belong! I am a member of the Family."

Many the babies and grownups here from photographs made in sixty-eight nations round our planet Earth. You travel and see what the camera saw. The wonder of human mind, heart, wit and instinct, is here. You might catch yourself saying, "I'm not a stranger here."

People! flung wide and far, born into toil, struggle, blood and dreams, among lovers, eaters, drinkers, workers, loafers, fighters, players, gamblers. Here are ironworkers, bridgemen, musicians, sandhogs, miners, builders of huts and skyscrapers, jungle hunters, landlords and the landless, the loved and the unloved, the lonely and abandoned, the brutal and the compassionate—one big family hugging close to the ball of Earth for its life and being.

Here or there you may witness a startling harmony where you say, "This will be haunting me a long time with a loveliness I hope to understand better."

In a seething of saints and sinners, winners or losers, in a womb of superstition, faith, genius, crime, sacrifice, here is the People, the one and only source of armies, navies, work-gangs, the living flowing breath of the history of nations, ever lighted by the reality or illusion of hope. Hope is a sustaining human gift.

Everywhere is love and love-making, weddings and babies from generation to generation keeping the Family of Man alive and continuing. Everywhere the sun, moon and stars, the climates and weathers, have meanings for people. Though meanings vary, we are alike in all countries and tribes in trying to read what sky, land and sea say to us. Alike and ever alike we are on all continents in the need of love, food, clothing, work, speech, worship, sleep, games, dancing, fun. From tropics to arctics humanity lives with these needs so alike, so inexorably alike.

Hands here, hands gnarled as thorntree roots and others soft as faded rose leaves. Hands reaching, praying and groping, hands holding tools, torches, brooms, fishnets, hands doubled in fists of flaring anger, hands moving in caress of beloved faces. The hands and feet of children playing ring-around-a-rosy—countries and languages different but the little ones alike in playing the same game.

Here are set forth babies arriving, suckling, growing into youths restless and questioning. Then as grownups they seek and hope. They mate, toil, fish, quarrel, sing, fight, pray, on all parallels and meridians having likeness. The earliest man, ages ago, had tools, weapons, cattle, as seen in his cave drawings. And like him the latest man of our day has his tools, weapons, cattle. The earliest man struggled through inexpressibly dark chaos of hunger, fear, violence, sex. A long journey it has been from that early Family of Man to the one of today which has become a still more prodigious spectacle.

If the human face is "the masterpiece of God" it is here then in a thousand fateful registrations. Often the faces speak what words can never say. Some tell of eternity and others only the latest tattlings. Child faces of blossom smiles or mouths of hunger are followed by homely faces of majesty carved and worn by love, prayer and hope, along with others light and carefree as thistledown in a late summer wind. Faces having land and sea on them, faces honest as the morning sun flooding a clean kitchen with light, faces crooked and lost and wondering where to go this afternoon or tomorrow morning. Faces in crowds, laughing and windblown leaf

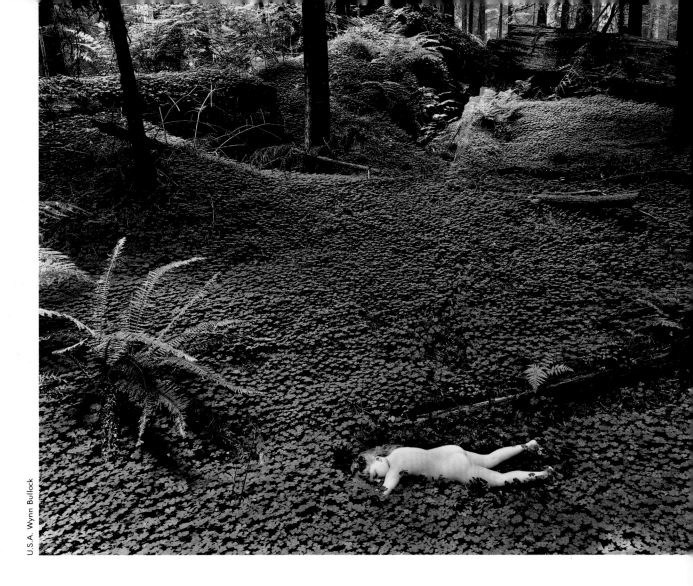

faces, profiles in an instant of agony, mouths in a dumbshow mockery lacking speech, faces of music in gay song or a twist of pain, a hate ready to kill, or calm and ready-for-death faces. Some of them are worth a long look now and deep contemplation later. Faces betokening a serene blue sky or faces dark with storm winds and lashing night rain. And faces beyond forgetting, written over with faiths in men and dreams of man surpassing himself. An alphabet here and a multiplication table of living breathing human faces.

In the times to come as in the past there will be generations taking hold as though loneliness and the genius of struggle has always dwelt in the hearts of pioneers. To the question, "What will the story be of the Family of Man across the near or far future?" some would reply, "For the answers read if you can the strange and baffling eyes of youth."

> There is only one man in the world
> and his name is All Men.
> There is only one woman in the world
> and her name is All Women.
> There is only one child in the world
> and the child's name is All Children.

A camera testament, a drama of the grand canyon of humanity, an epic woven of fun, mystery and holiness—here is the Family of Man!

*Carl Sandburg*

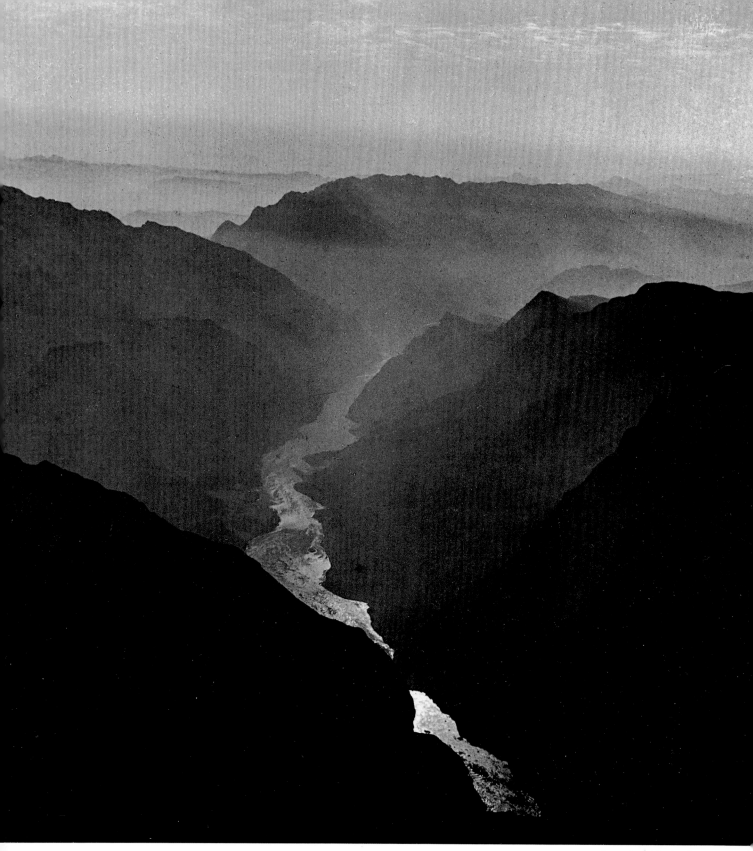

China. Dmitri Kessel  *Life*

*. . .and then I asked him with my eyes to ask again yes*

*and then he asked me would I yes . . .*

*and first I put my arms around him yes*

*and drew him down to me so he could feel my breasts all perfume yes*

*and his heart was going like mad*

*and yes I said yes I will Yes.*

James Joyce

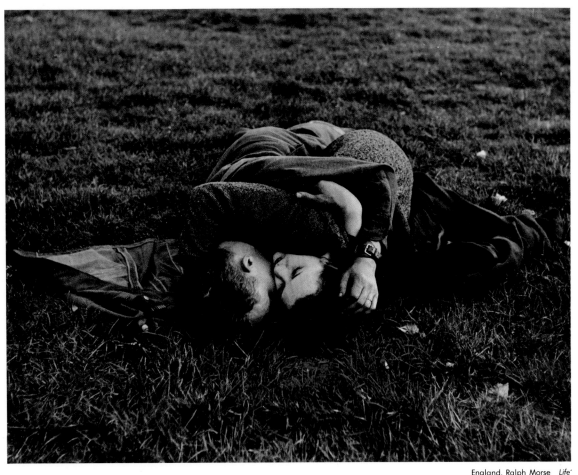

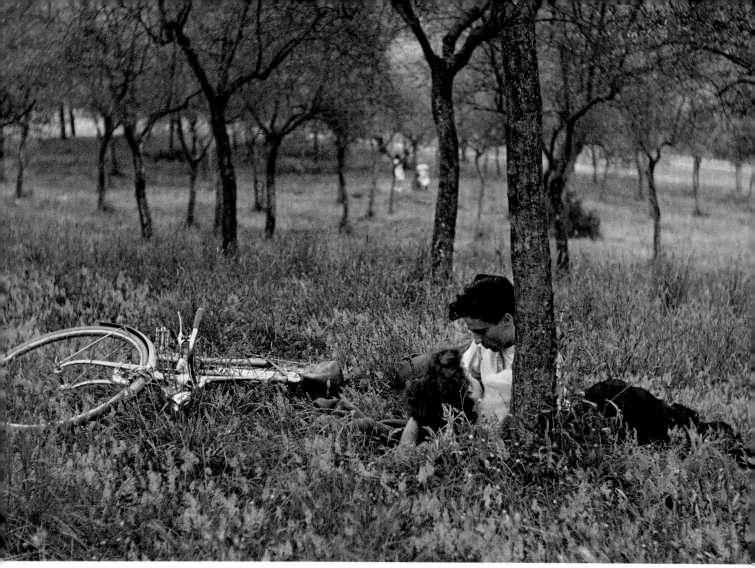

Italy. Gotthard Schuh

New Guinea. Laurence LeGuay

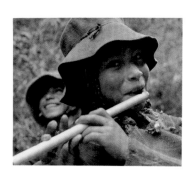

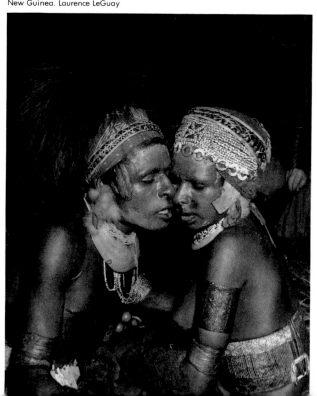

8

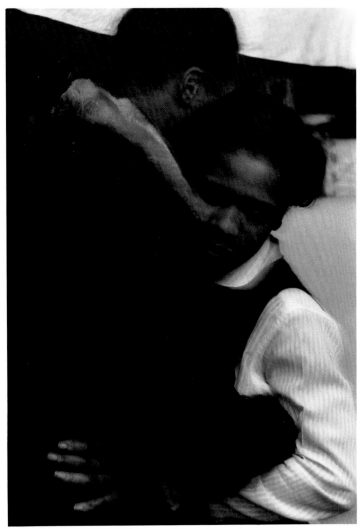

U.S.A. Roy De Carava

U.S.A. Louis Faurer

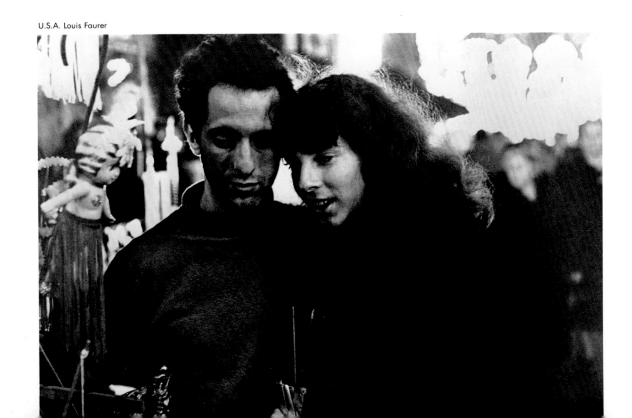

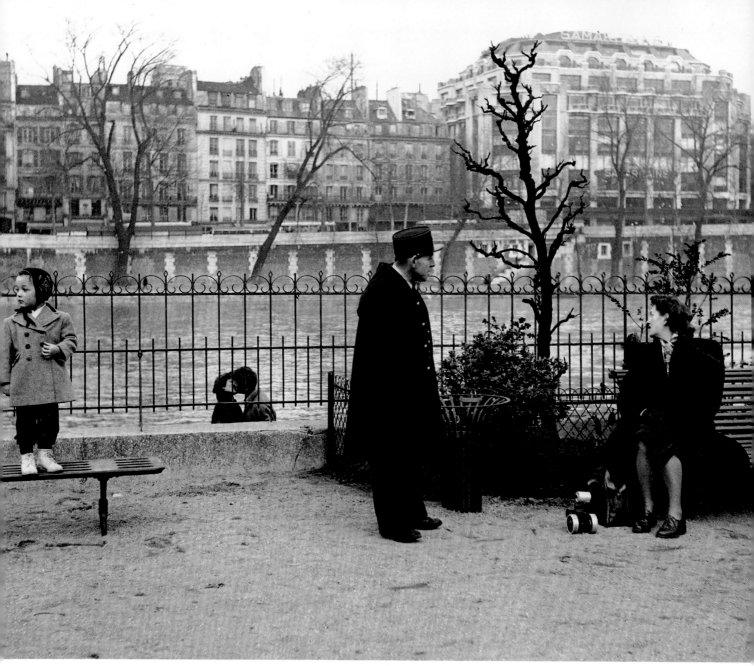

France. Robert Doisneau  *Rapho Guillumette*

France. Robert Doisneau  *Rapho Guillumette*

U.S.A. Lou Bernstein

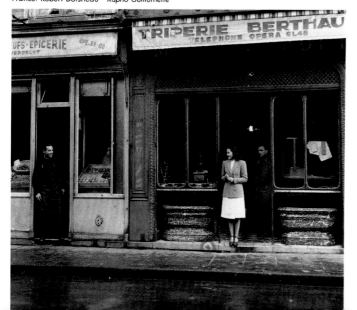

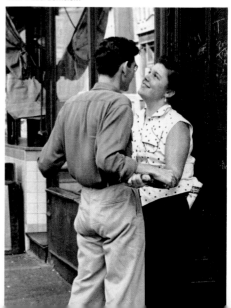

10

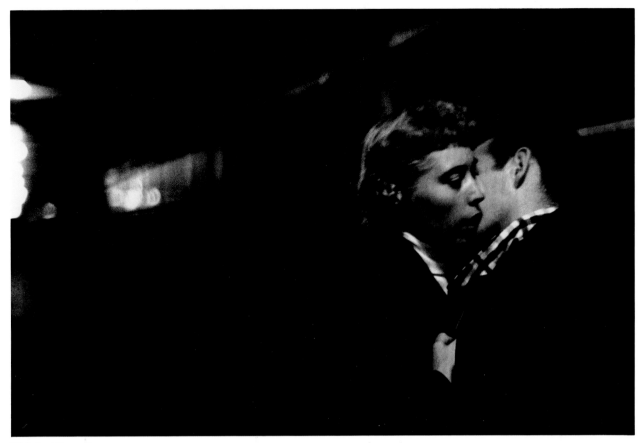

U.S.A. Ernst Haas  *Magnum*

U.S.A. Louis Faurer

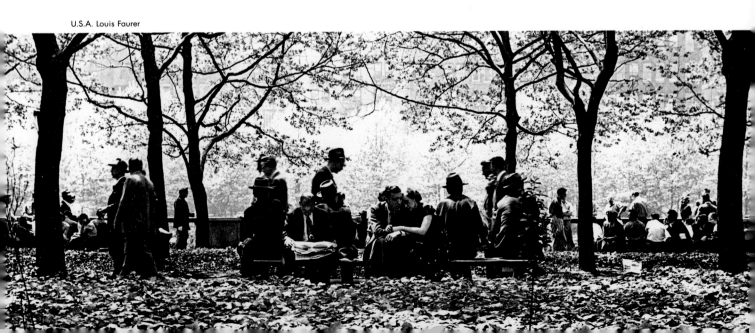

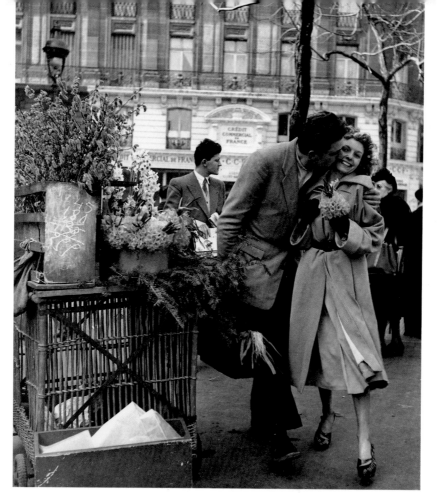

France. Robert Doisneau *Rapho Guillumette*

U.S.A. David Linton

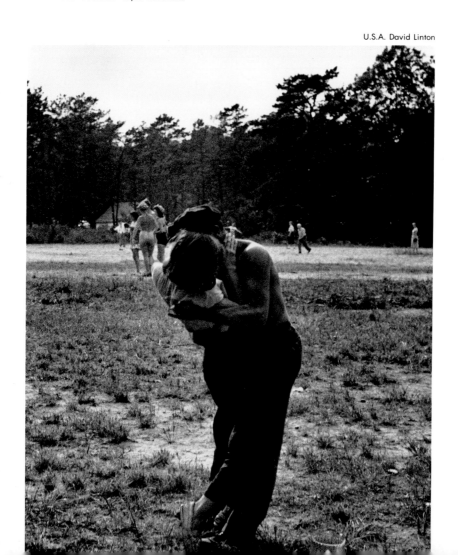

U.S.A. Wayne Miller

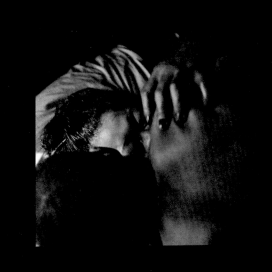

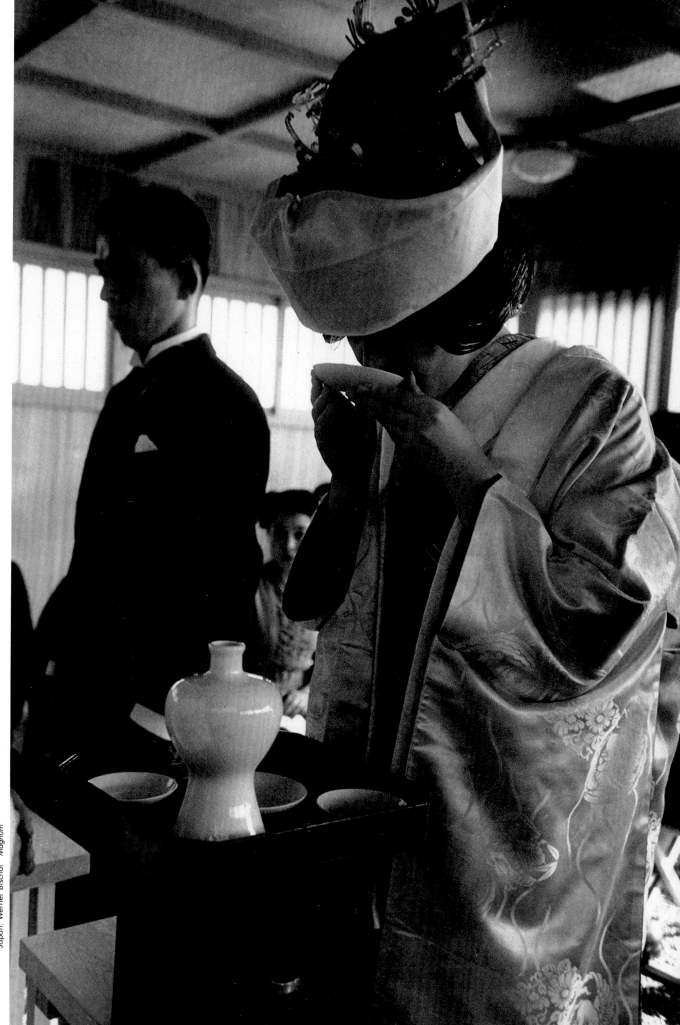

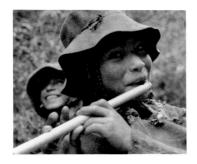

*We shall be one person*     Pueblo Indian

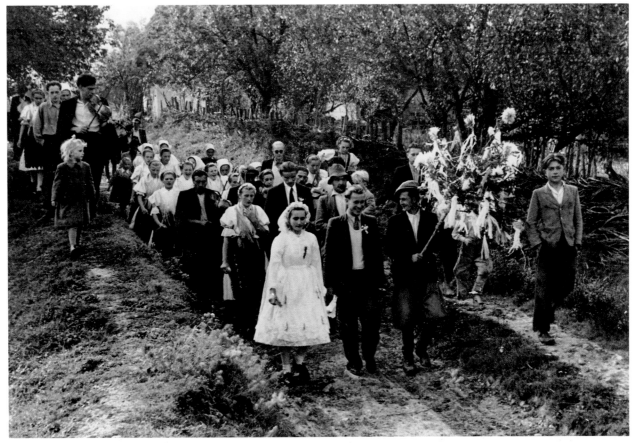

Czechoslovakia. Robert Capa    *Magnum*

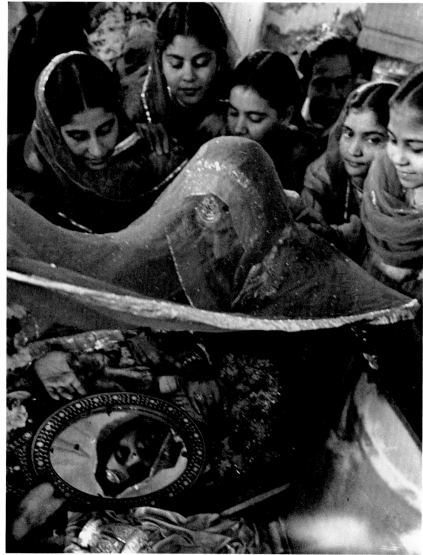

India. Frank Horvat  *Black Star*

Sweden. Hans Malmberg

U.S.A. Jay Te Winburn  *Vogue*

France. Henri Cartier-Bresson  *Magnum*

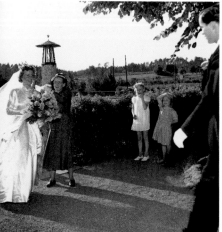

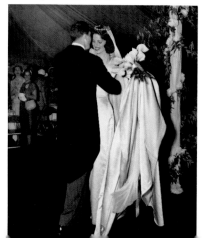

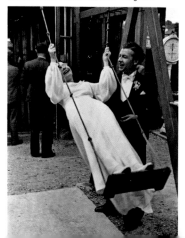

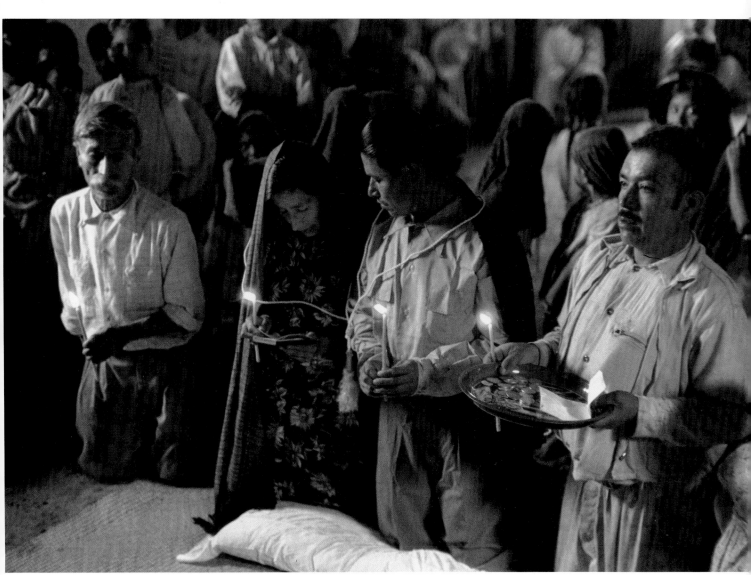

Mexico. Wayne Miller  *Life*

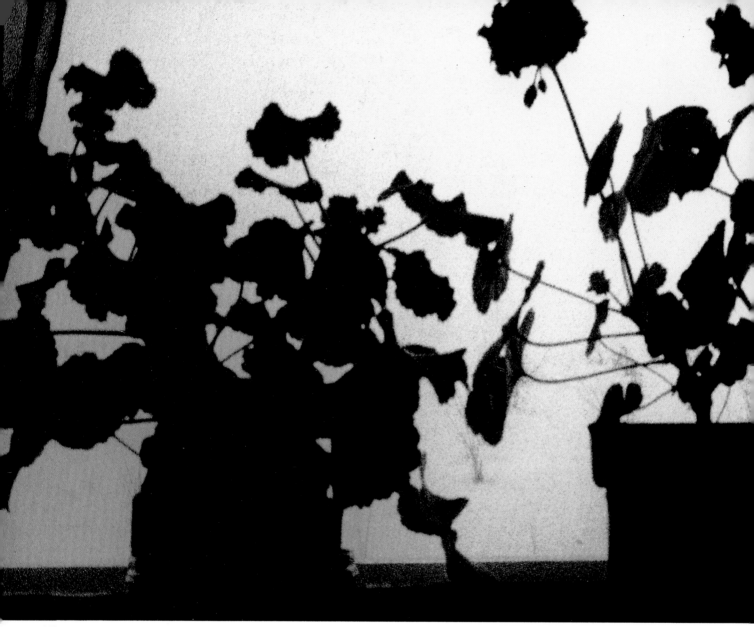

U.S.A. Paul Himmel

U.S.A. Margery Lewis

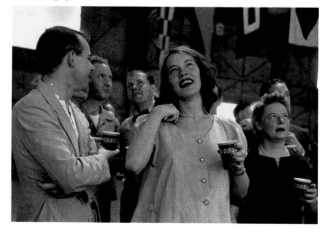

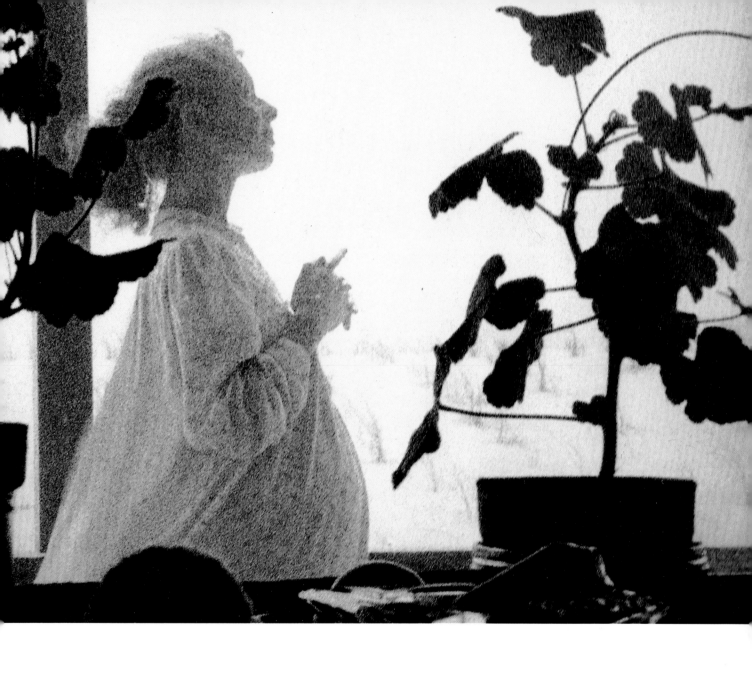

U.S.A. Elliott Erwitt *Magnum*

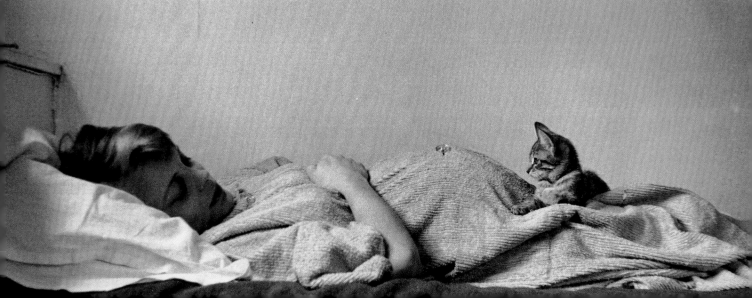

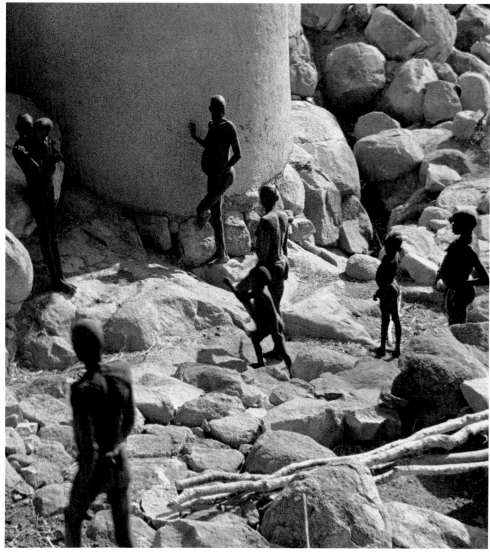

Kordofan. George Rodger  *Magnum*

Japan. Hideo Haga

U.S.A. Robert Frank

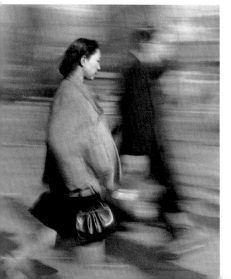

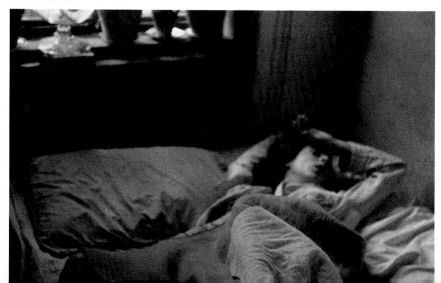

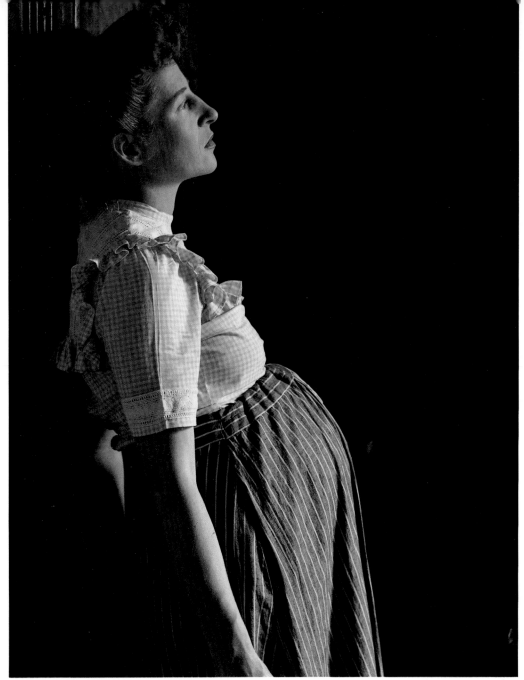

Mexico. Manuel Alvarez Bravo

U.S.A. Robert Frank

Arctic. Richard Harrington  *Three Lions*

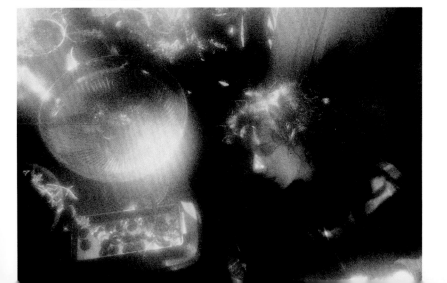

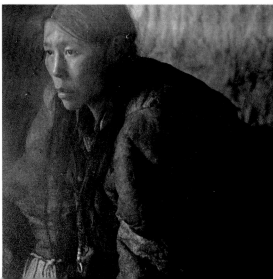

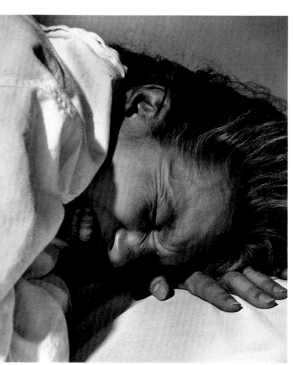

U.S.A. Wayne Miller

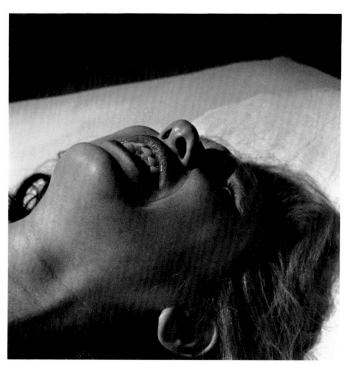

U.S.A. Wayne Miller

*The universe resounds with the joyful cry I am.*

Scriabin

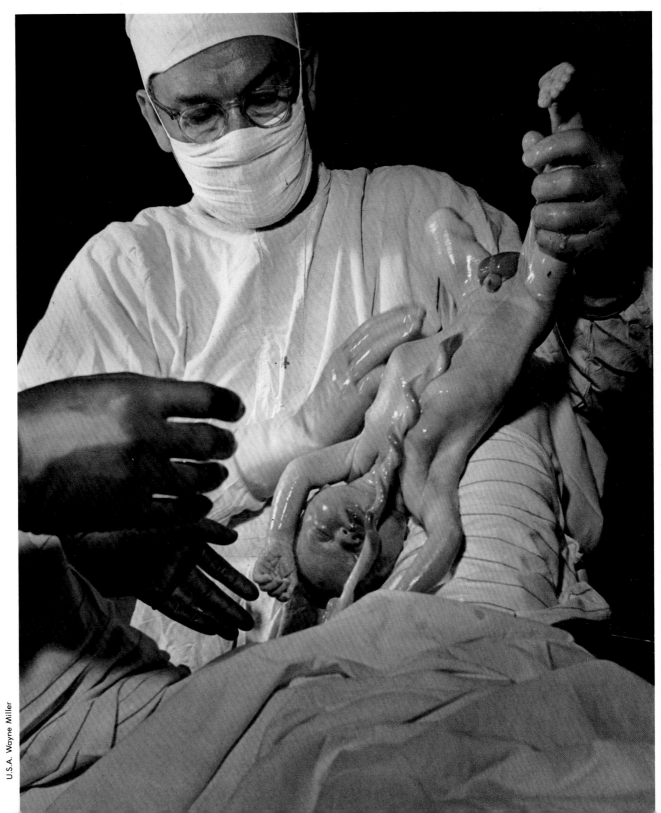

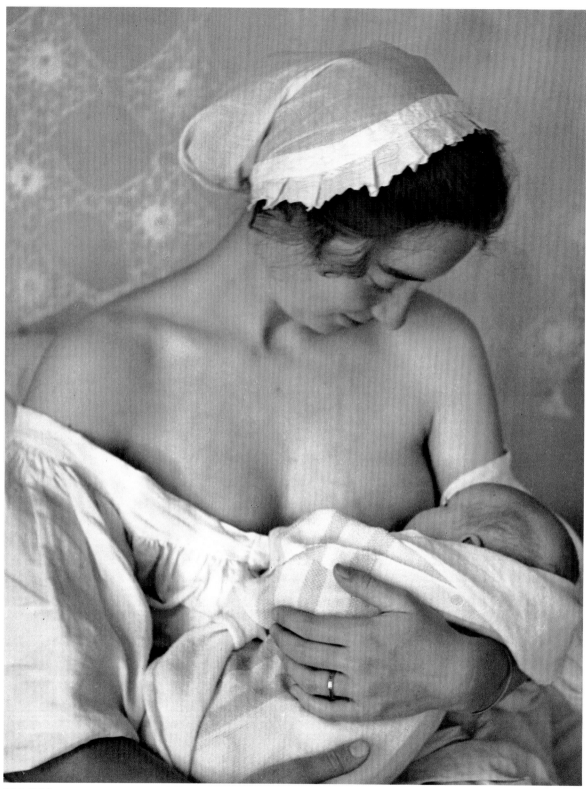

U.S.A. Nell Dorr

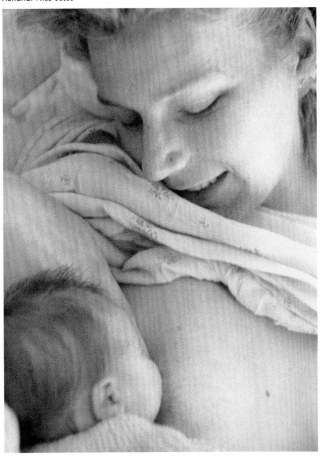

*And shall not loveliness be loved forever?*     Euripides

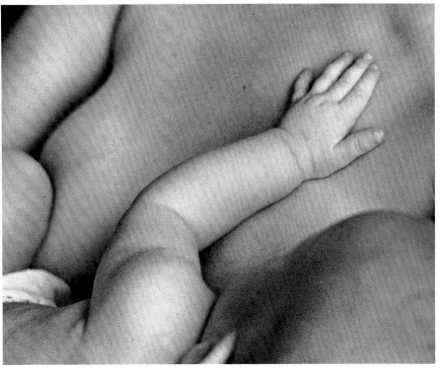

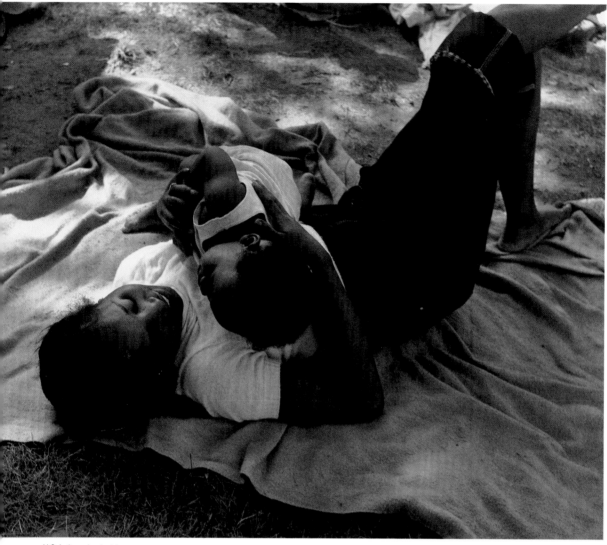

U.S.A. Leon Levinstein

India. Gitel Steed

Australia. David Moore

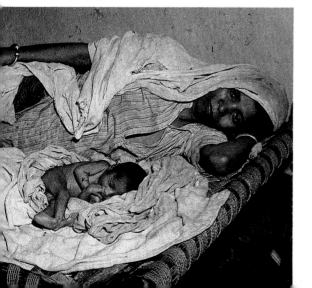

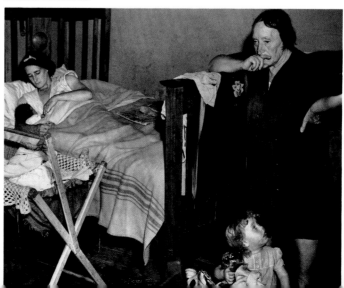

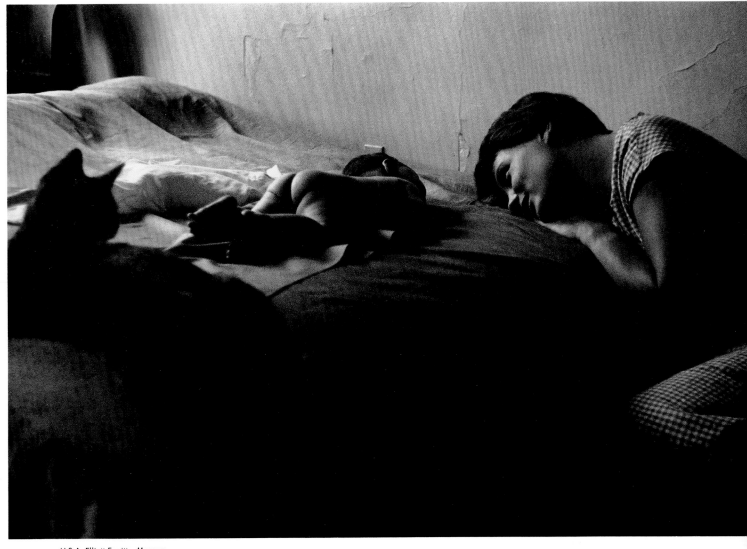

U.S.A. Elliott Erwitt *Magnum*

*Bone of my bones, and flesh of my flesh . . .*     Genesis 2:23

Japan. Eiju Otaki *Ars Camera*

U.S.A. Wayne Miller

India. Gitel Steed

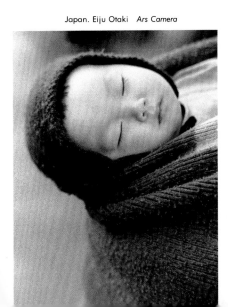
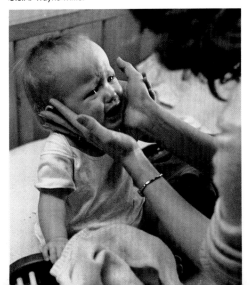
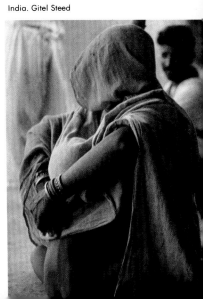

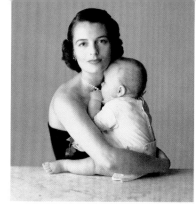

U.S.A. Irving Penn  *Vogue*

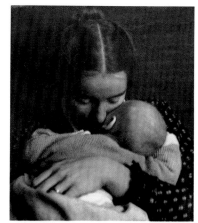

U.S.A. Nell Dorr

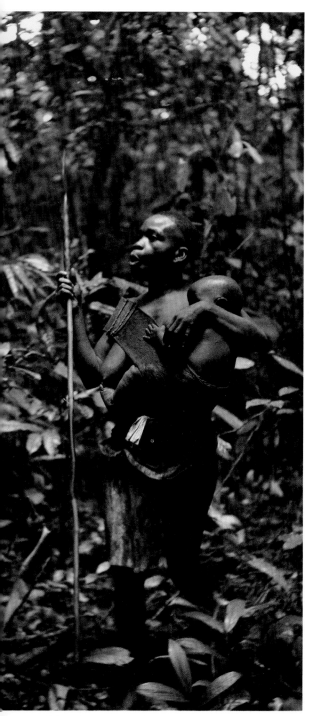

Belgian Congo. Lennart Nilsson  *Black Star*

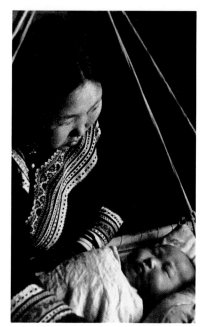

Siberia. Sovfoto

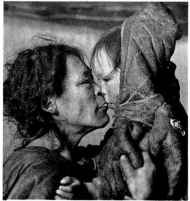

Arctic. Richard Harrington  *Three Lions*

28

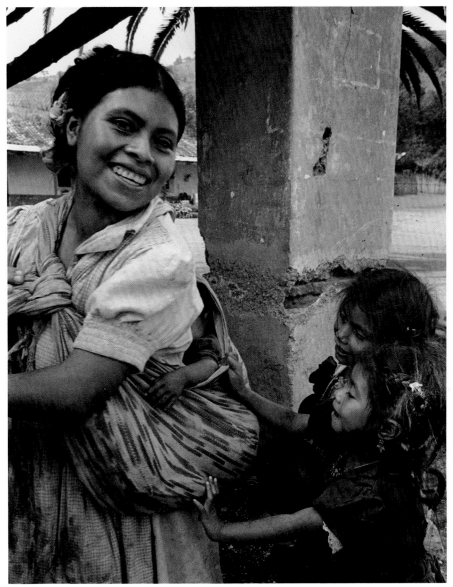

Guatemala. Lisa Larsen  *Life*

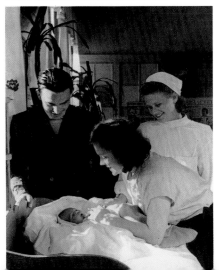

China. Chien Hao

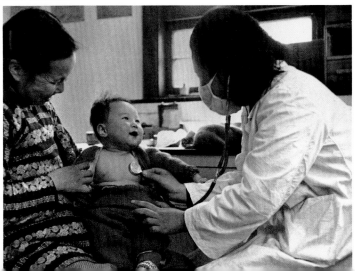

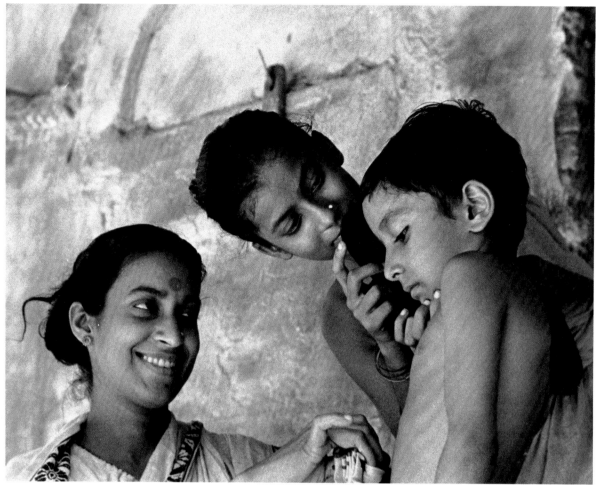

India. Satyajit Ray

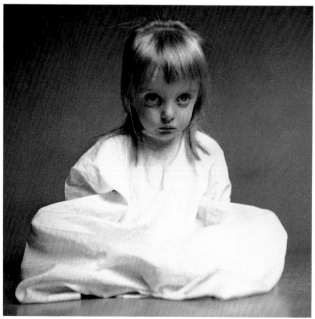

U.S.A. Irving Penn  Vogue

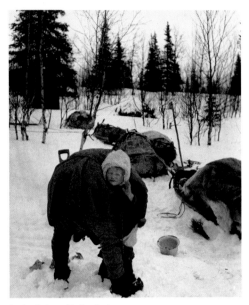

Lapland. Anna Riwkin-Brick

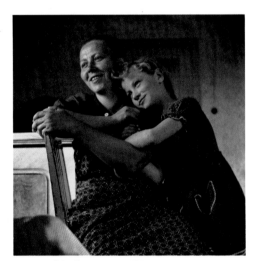

Austria. Ted Castle   Magnum, AFSC

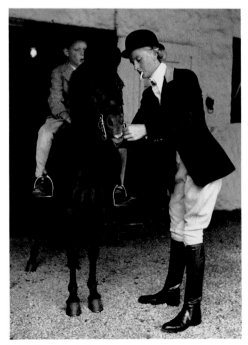

U.S.A. Constantin Joffé   Vogue

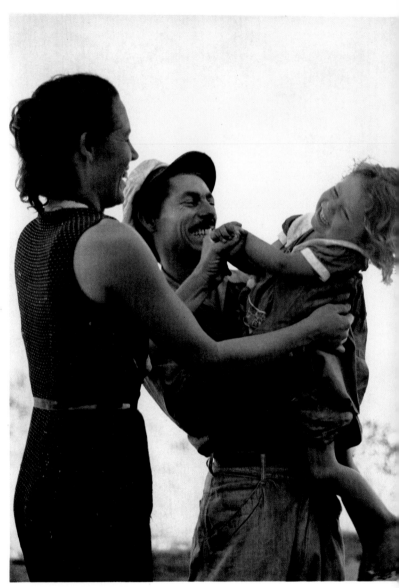

Cuba. Eve Arnold   Magnum

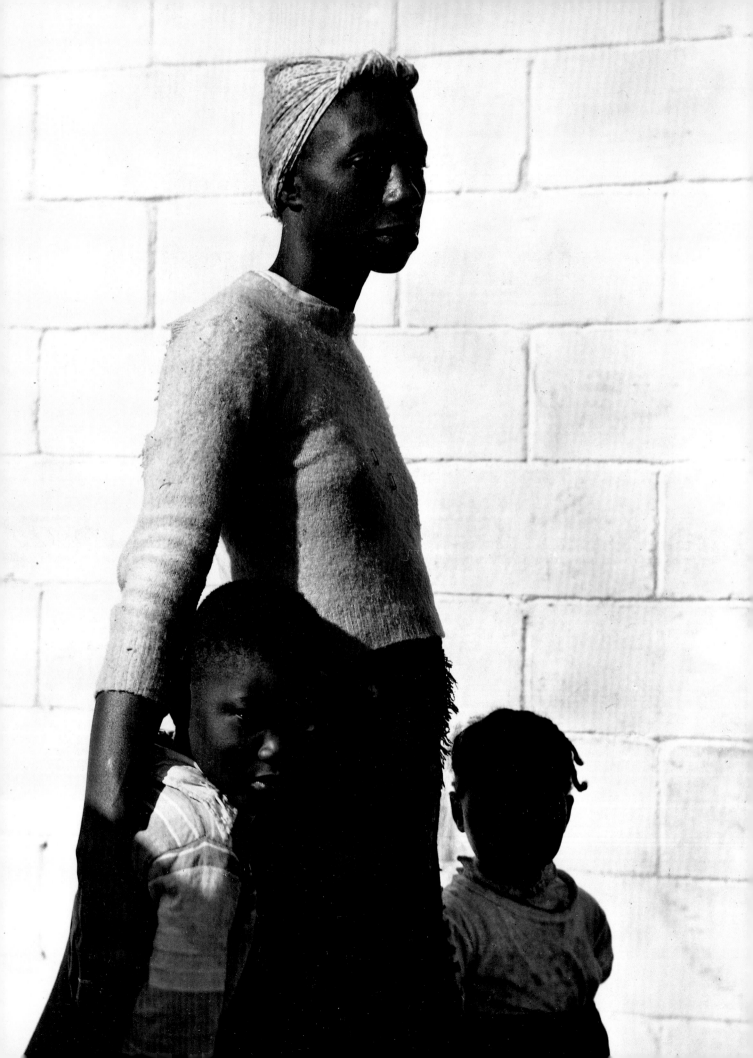

*She is a tree of life to them . . .*

Proverbs 3:18

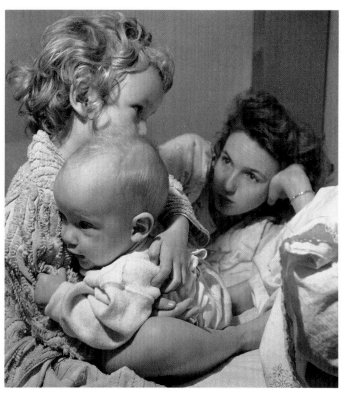

U.S.A. Wayne Miller

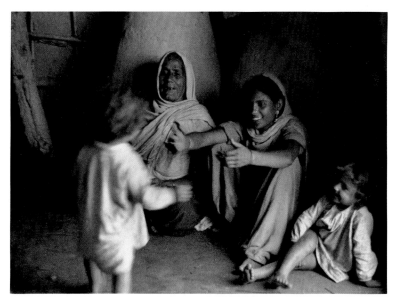

India. Eric Schwab   *UN*

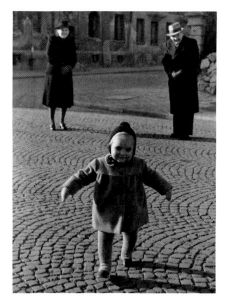

Germany. Hannes Rosenberg

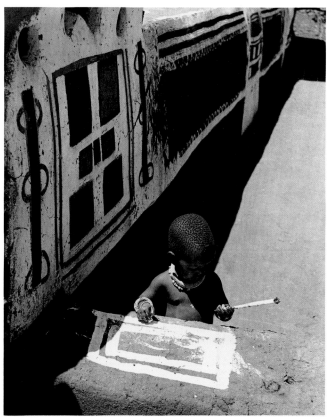

South Africa. Constance Stuart   *Black Star*

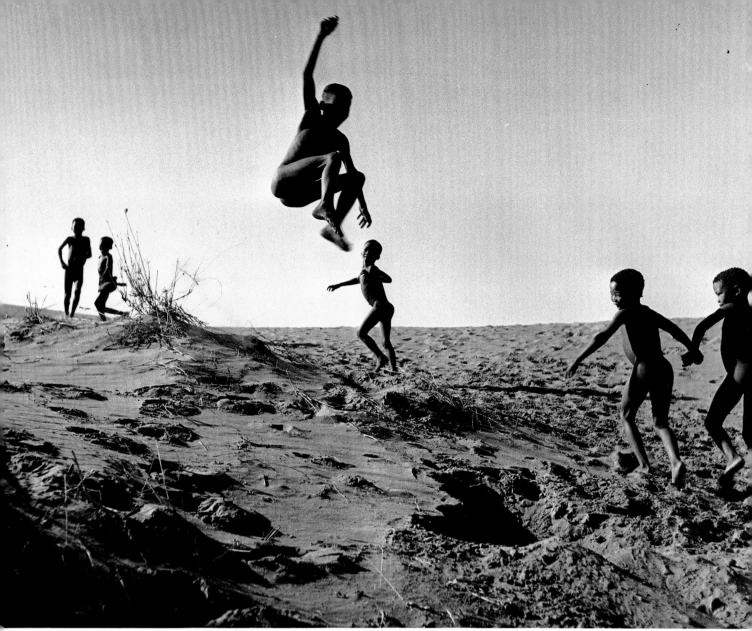

Bechuanaland. Nat Farbman *Life*

*The little ones leaped, and shouted, and laugh'd*

*And all the hills echoed . . .*

William Blake

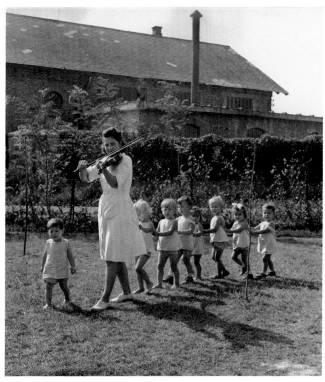

Austria. David Seymour  *Magnum, UNESCO*

U.S.A. Alfred Eisenstaedt  *Life*

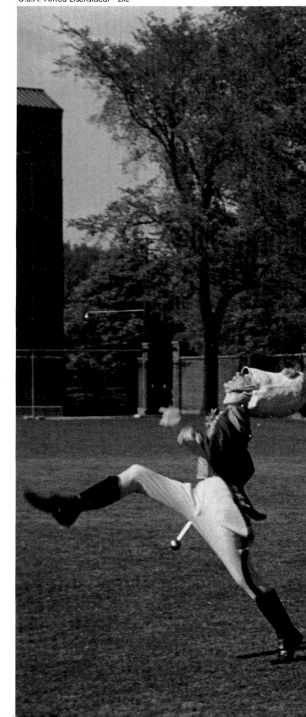

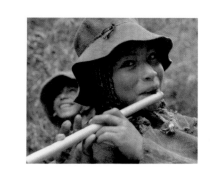

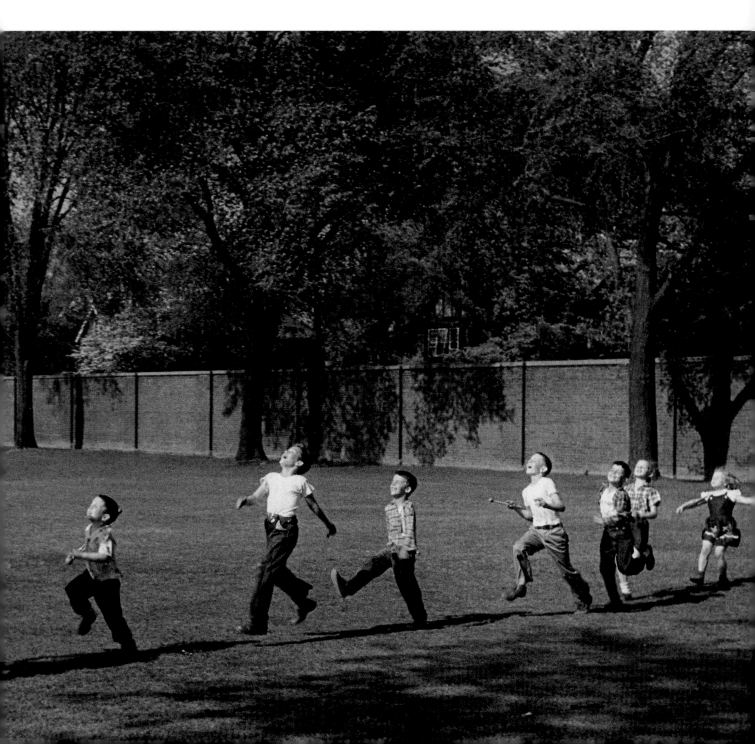

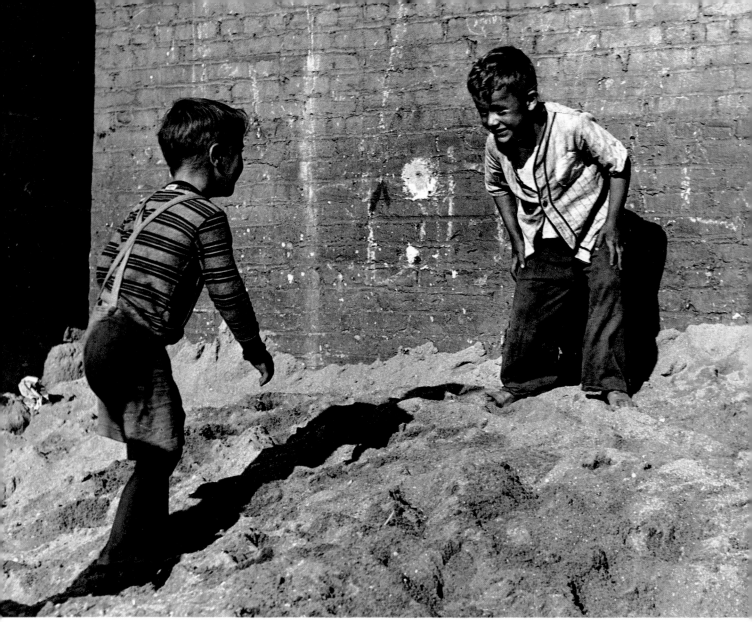

U.S.A. Arthur Leipzig

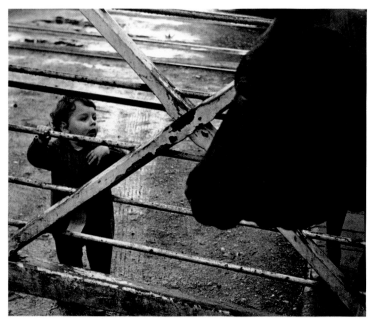

England. Ian Smith  *Life*

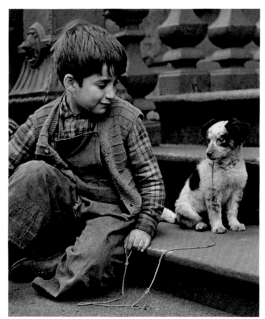

U.S.A. Clemens Kalischer

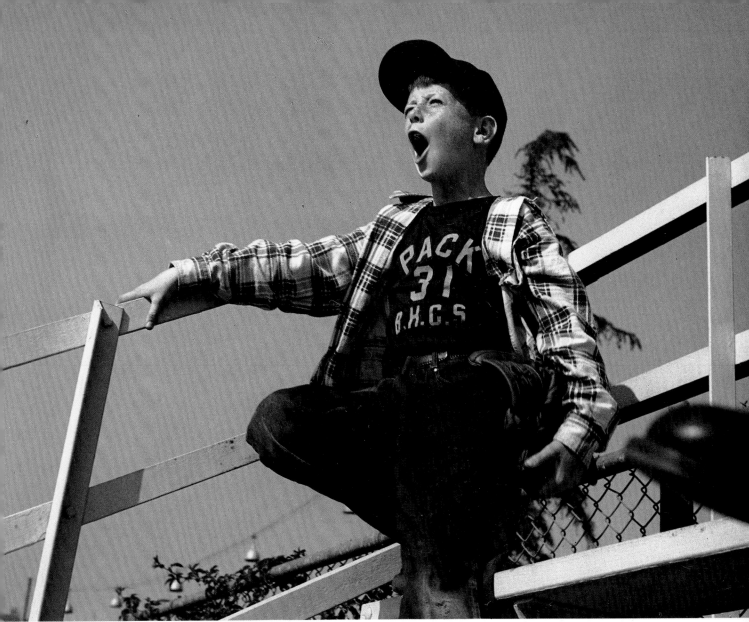

U.S.A. Shirley Burden

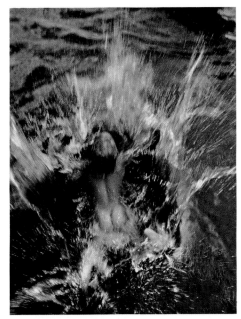

U.S.A. Edward Steichen

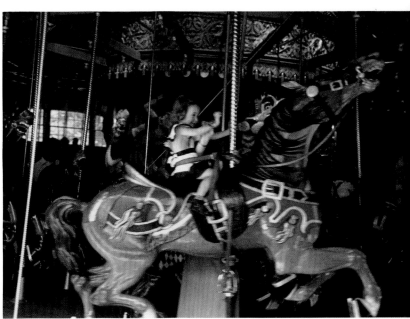

U.S.A. Burt Glinn  *Magnum, Life*

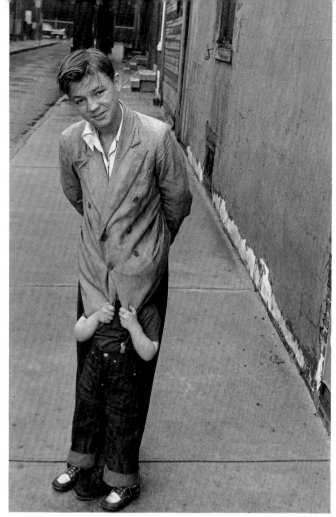

U.S.A. Edward Wallowitch

U.S.A. Yasuhiro Ishimoto

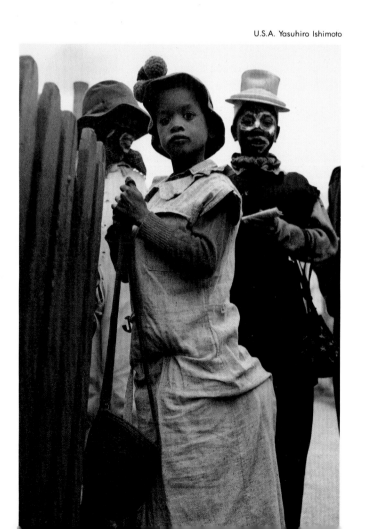

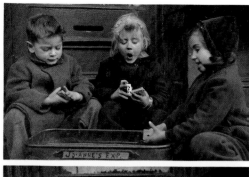

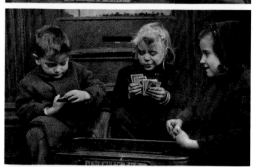

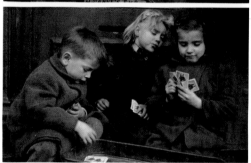

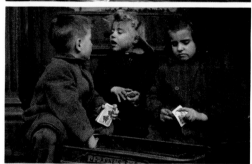

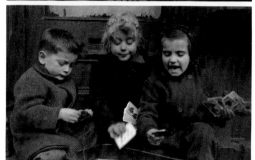

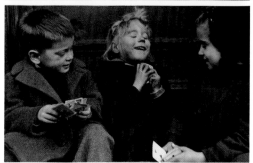

U.S.A. Ruth Orkin

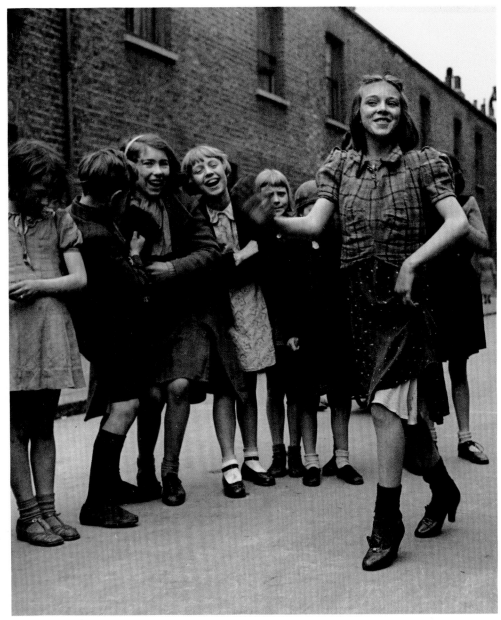

England. Bill Brandt

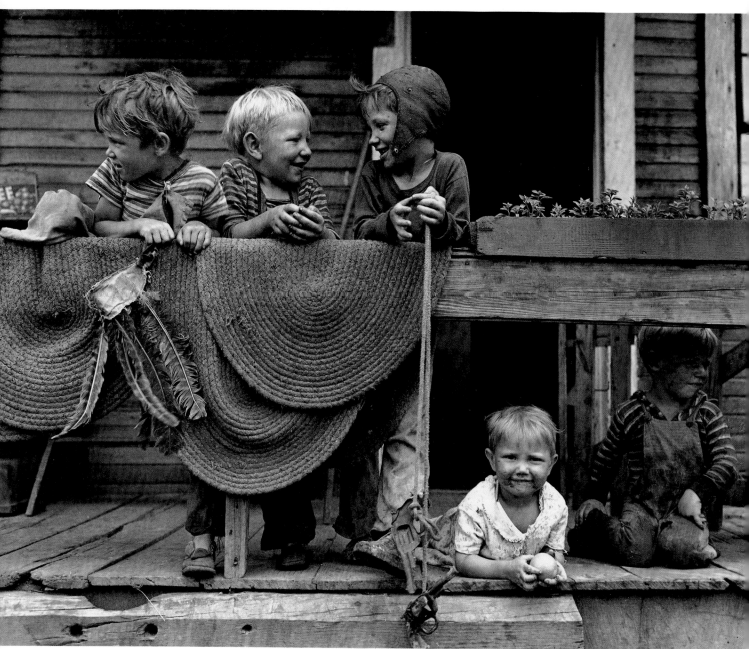

U.S.A. Russell Lee  *Bureau of Mines*

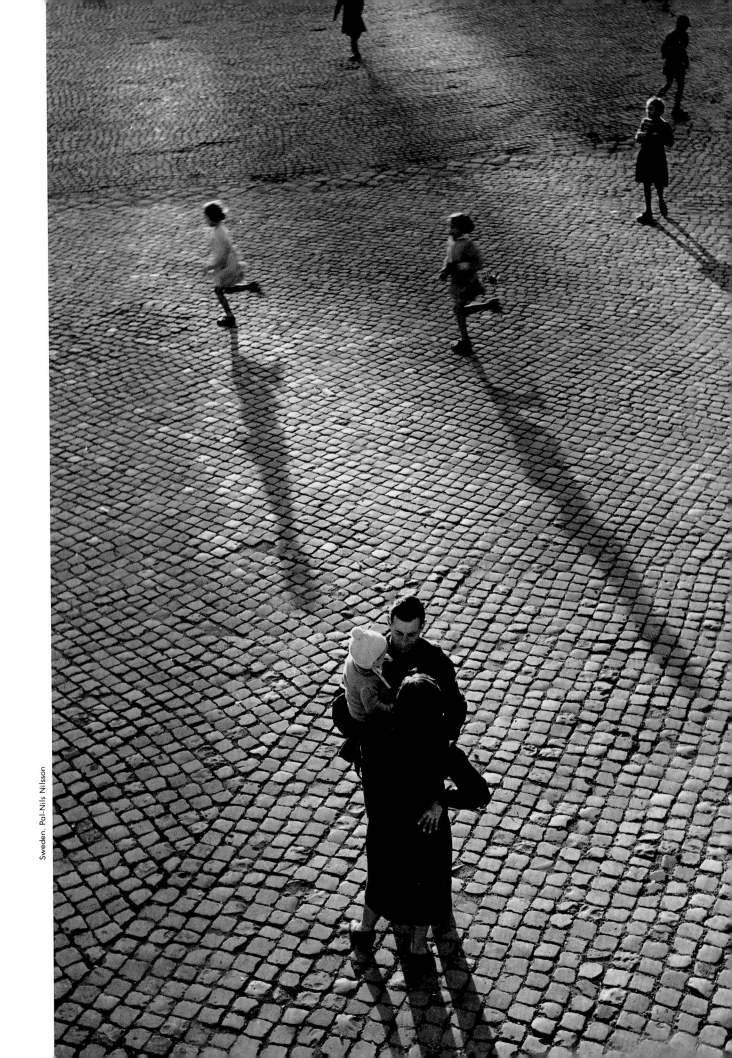

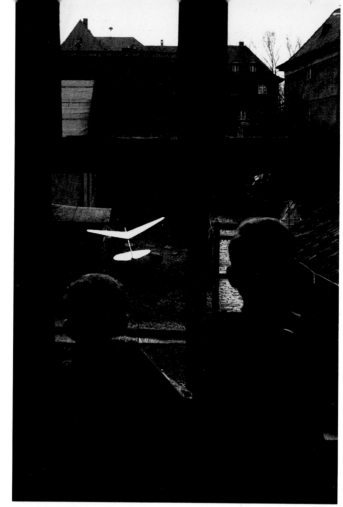

Germany. Carl Mydans  *Life*

France. Willy Ronis

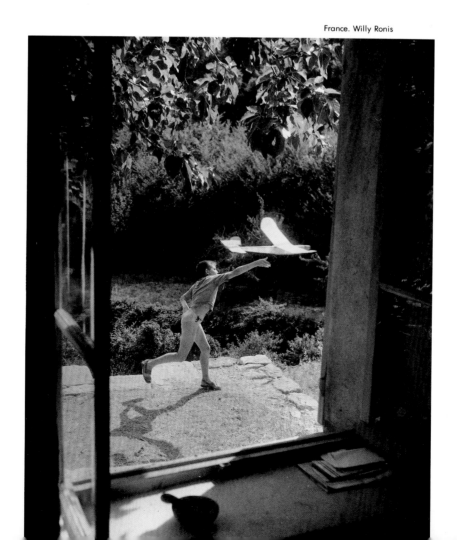

44

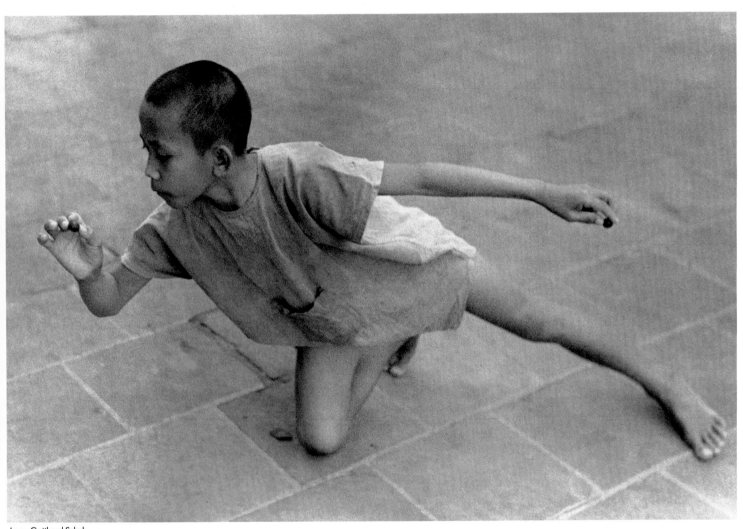

Java. Gotthard Schuh

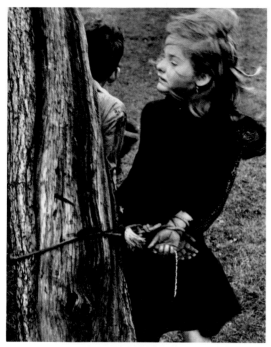

U.S.A. Yasuhiro Ishimoto

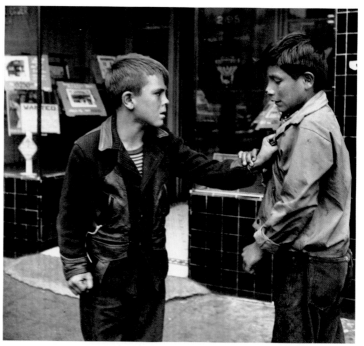

U.S.A. Homer Page

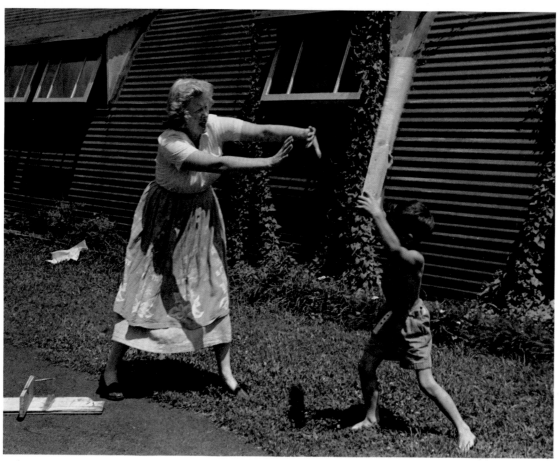

U.S.A. George Heyer  *Pix*

U.S.A. W. Eugene Smith

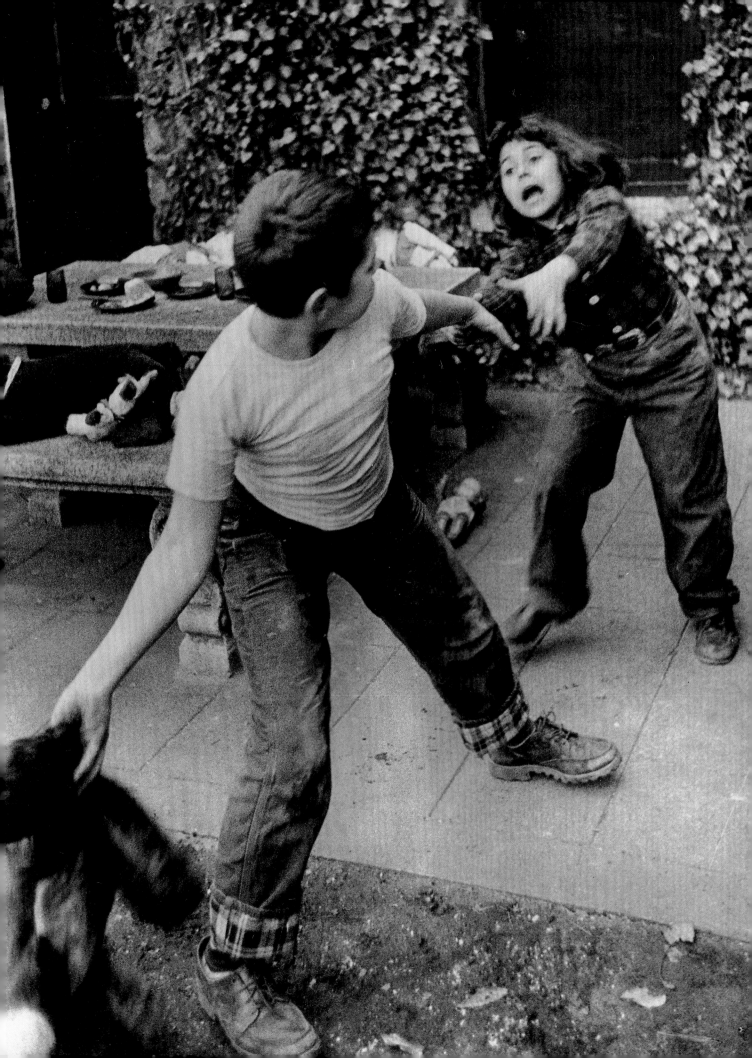

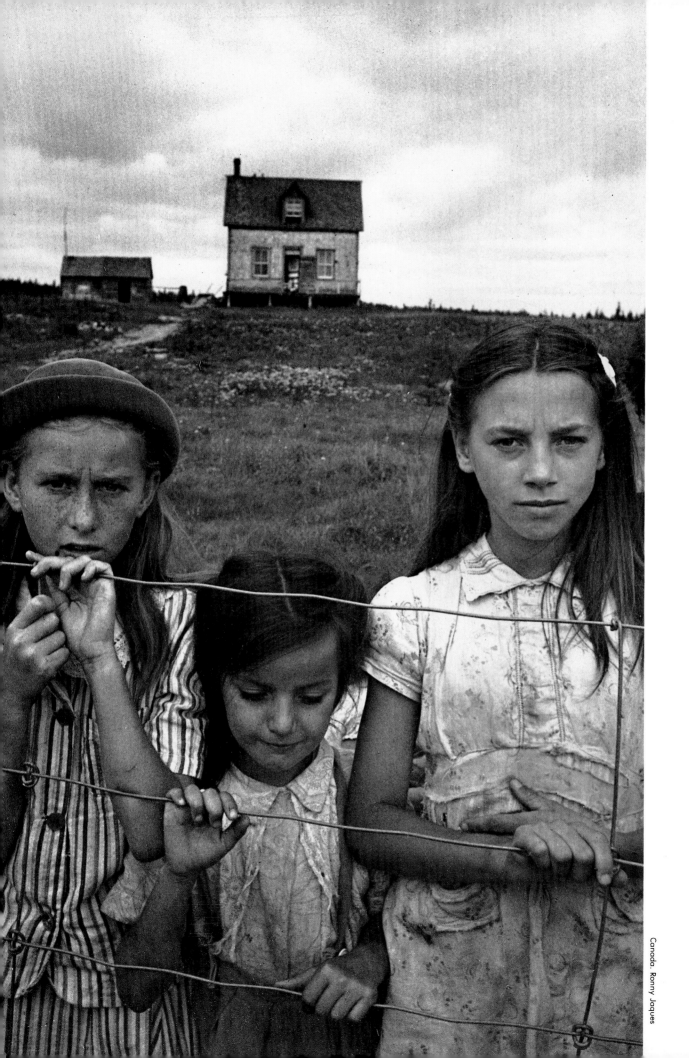

U.S.A. Leon Levinstein

U.S.A. Dorothea Lange  *Farm Security Adm.*

U.S.A. Dave Myers

Italy. U.S. Navy

U.S.A. Photographer unknown

Poland. Roman Vishniac

Canada. Ronny Jaques

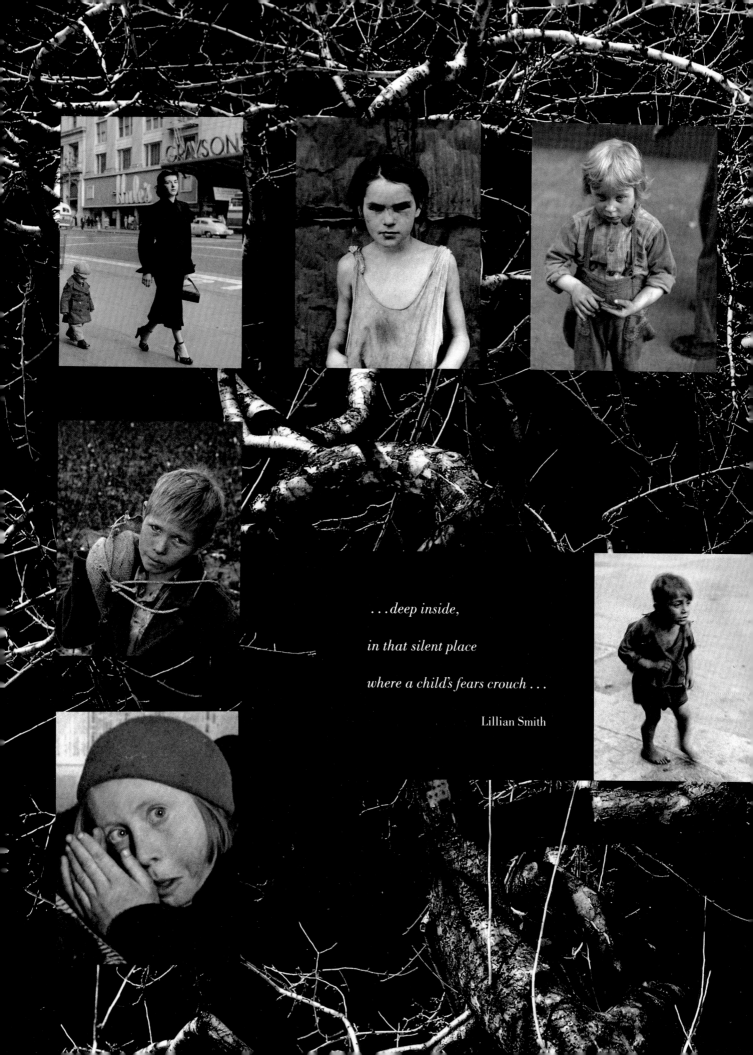

...deep inside,

in that silent place

where a child's fears crouch...

Lillian Smith

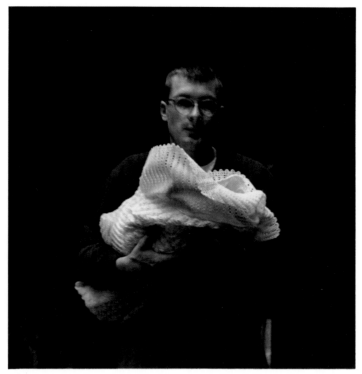

U.S.A. Dorothea Lange

*When I am a man, then I shall be a hunter*

*When I am a man, then I shall be a harpooner*

*When I am a man, then I shall be a canoe-builder*

*When I am a man, then I shall be a carpenter*

*When I am a man, then I shall be an artisan*

*Oh father! ya ha ha ha*

Kwakiutl Indian

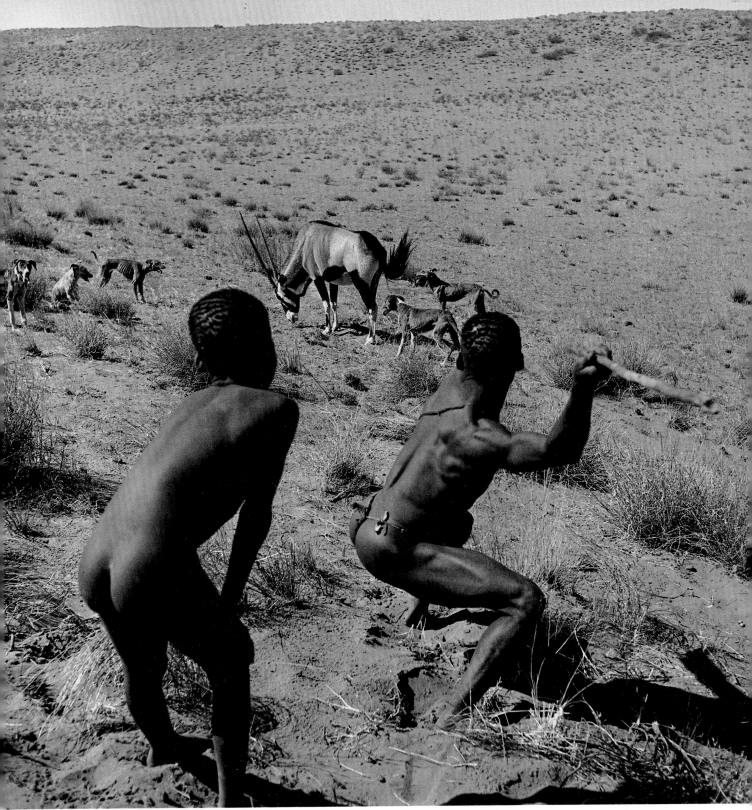

Bechuanaland. Nat Farbman  *Life*

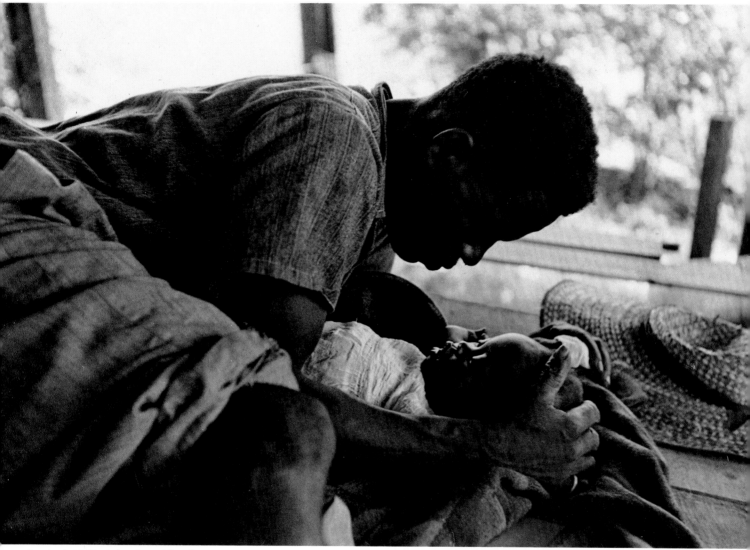

Jamaica, British West Indies. George Silk  *Life*

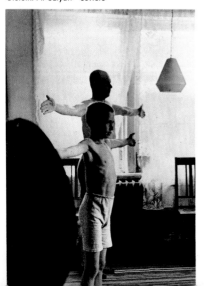

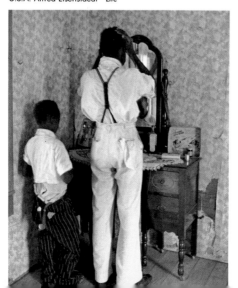

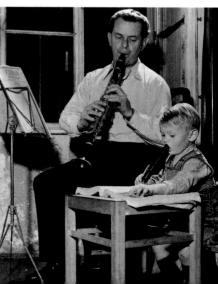

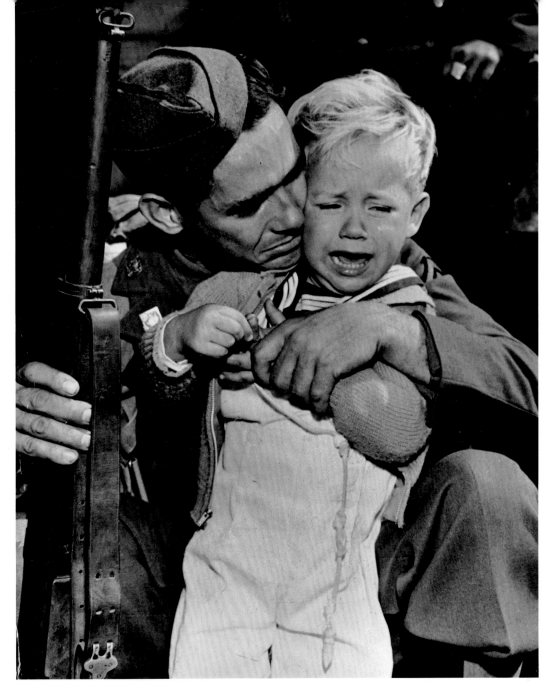

U.S.A. Bob Jakobsen  *Los Angeles Times*

U.S.A. Diane and Allan Arbus  *Vogue*

U.S.A. Martha Kitchen

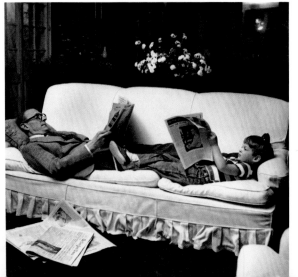

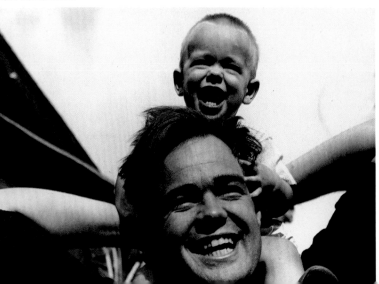

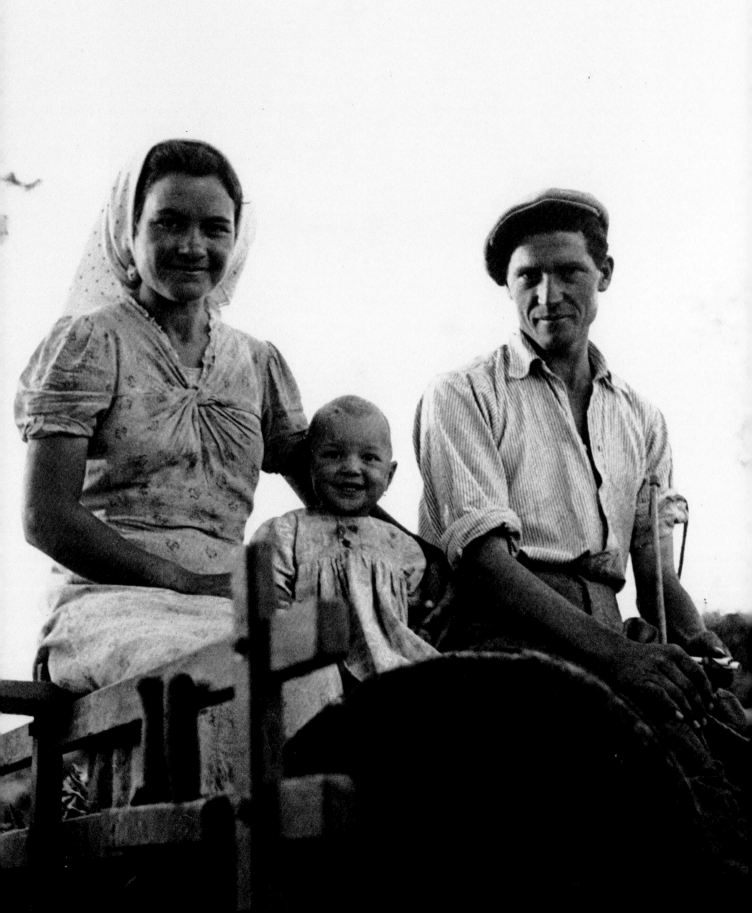

*With all beings and all things we shall be as relatives*

Sioux Indian

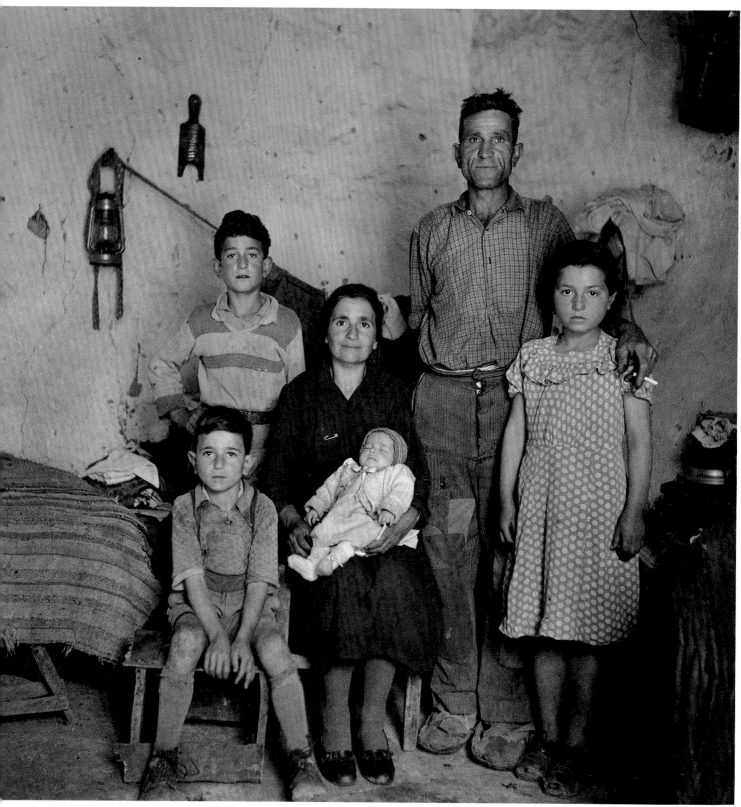

Sicily. Vito Fiorenza

56

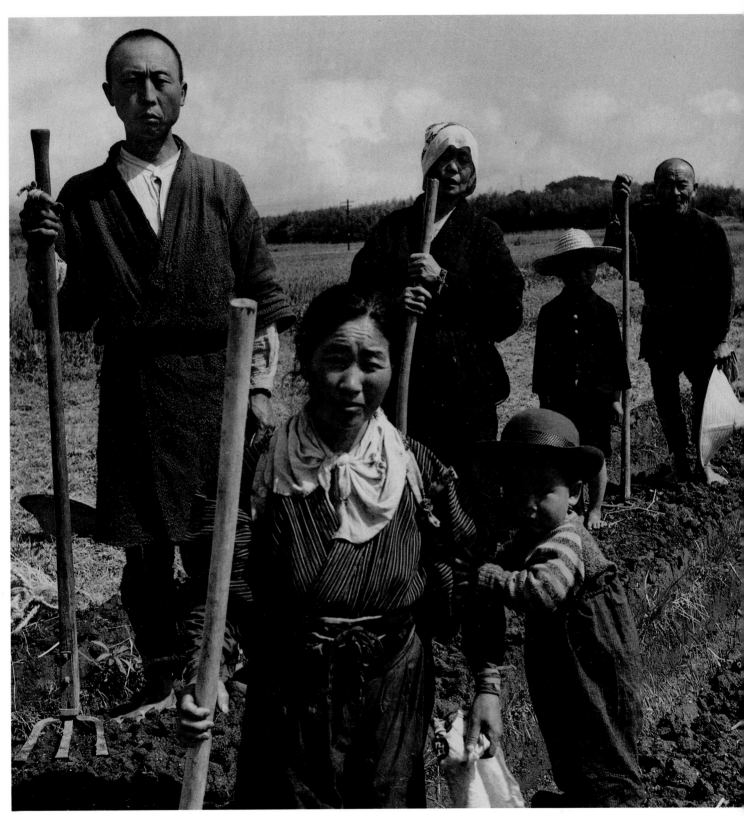

Japan. Carl Mydans  *Life*

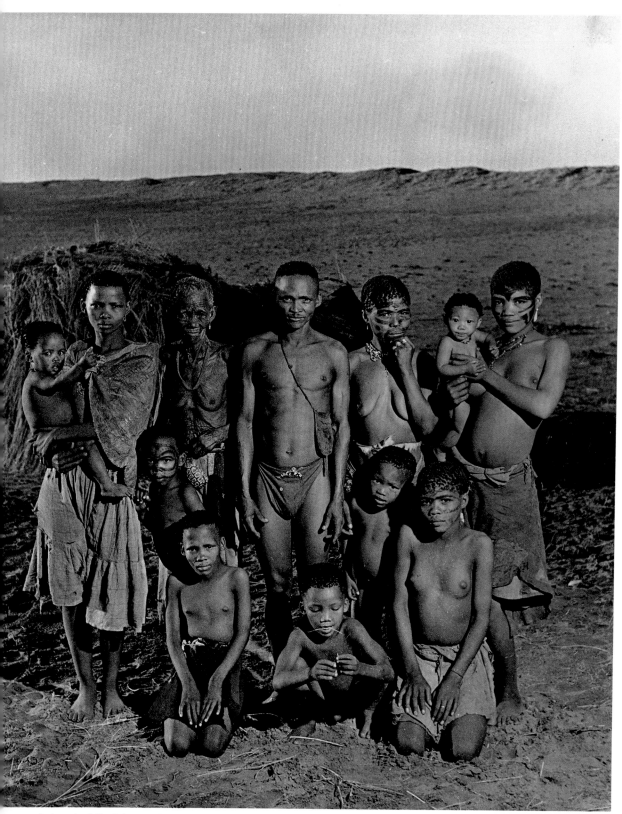

Bechuanaland. Nat Farbman  *Life*

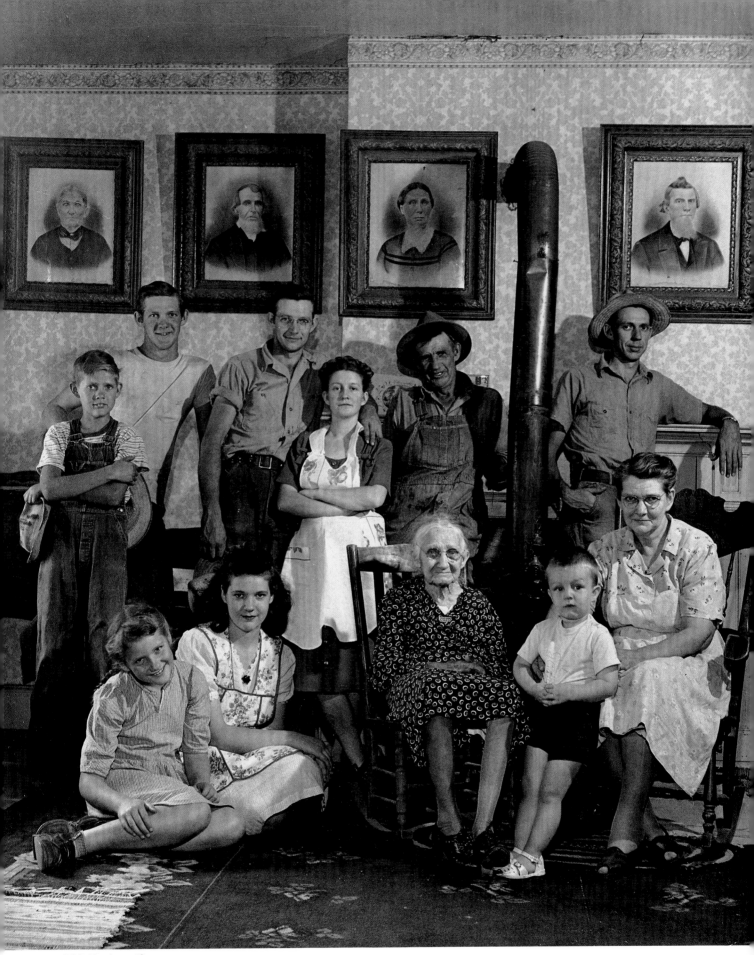

U.S.A. Nina Leen  *Life*

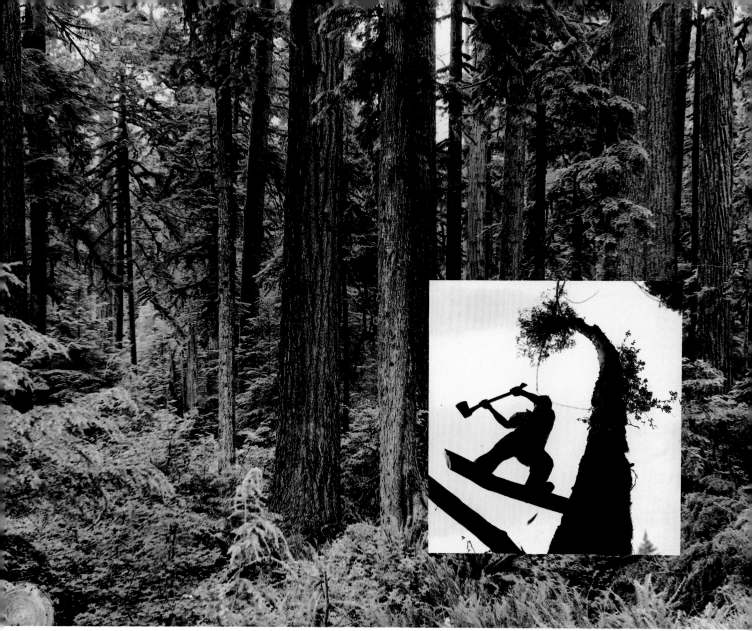

U.S.A. United States Dept. of the Interior

New Zealand. George Silk  *Life*

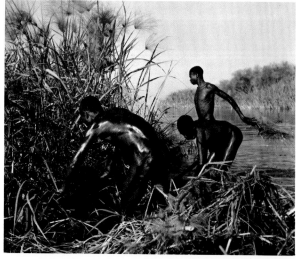

*Before me peaceful,*

*Behind me peaceful,*

*Under me peaceful,*

*Over me peaceful,*

*All around me peaceful . . .*

60                                          Navajo Indian

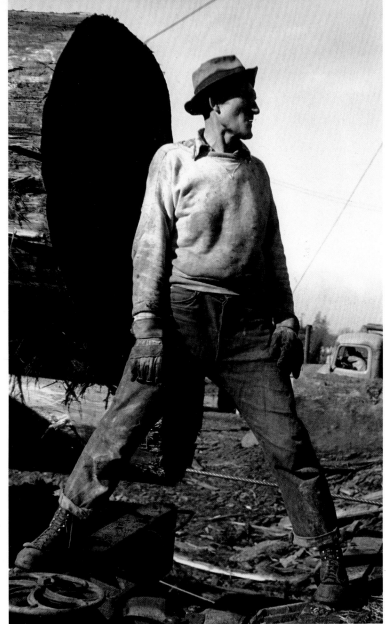

U.S.A. Homer Page

Bechuanaland. Nat Farbman *Life*

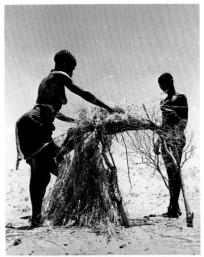

U.S.S.R. Robert Capa *Ladies' Home Journal*

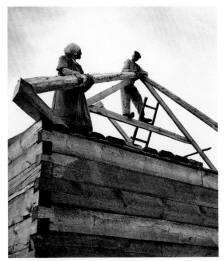

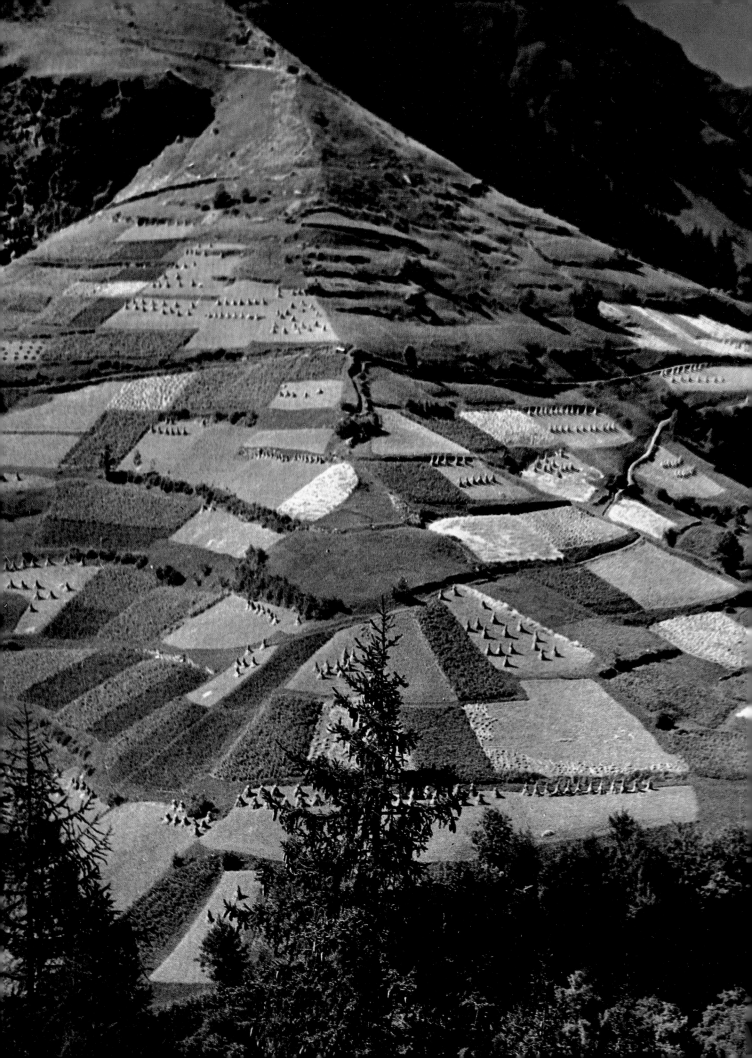

*The land is a mother that never dies*

Maori

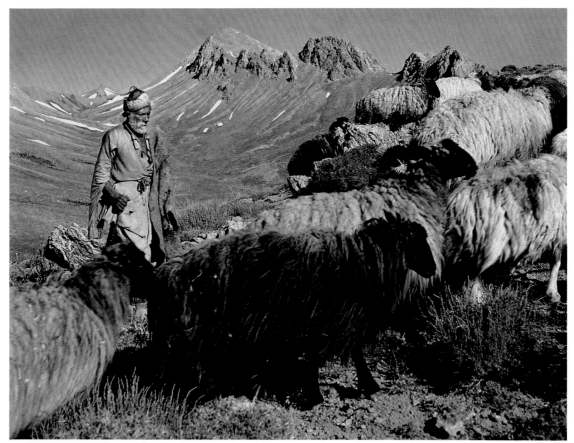

Iran. David Duncan  *Life*

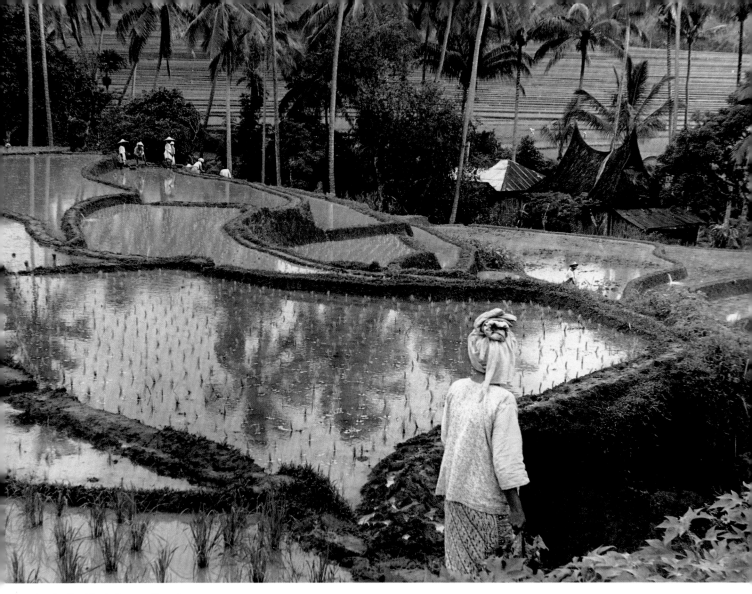

Indonesia. Henri Cartier-Bresson *Magnum*

Japan. Ihei Kimura

China. Li Shu

Japan. Shizuo Yamamoto

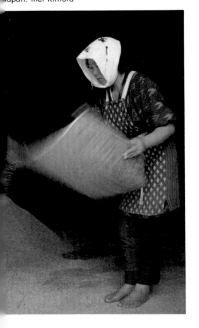

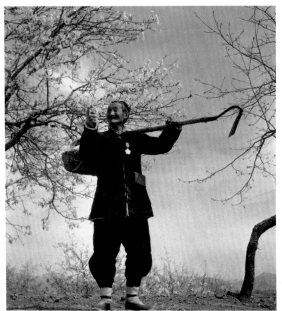

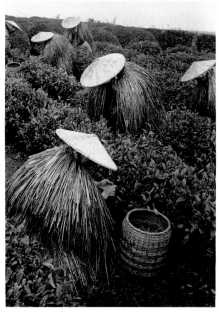

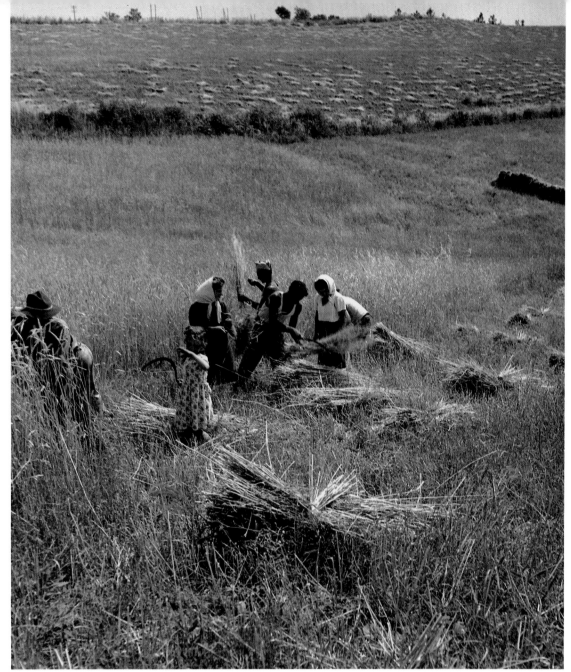

Italy. Dmitri Kessel  *Life*

China. Dmitri Kessel  *Life*

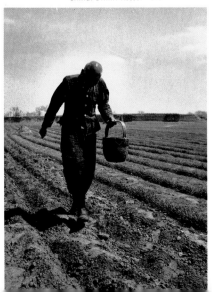

Ireland. G. H. Metcalf  *Black Star*

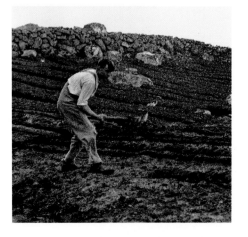

U.S.A. Dorothea Lange

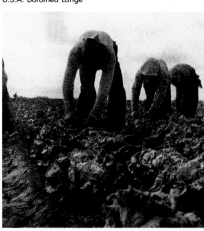

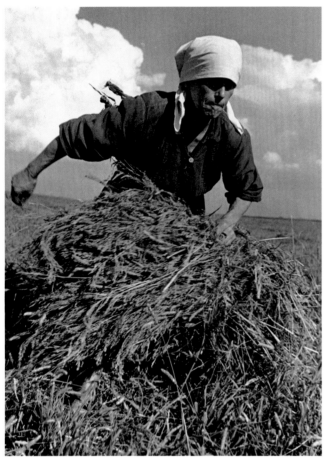

U.S.S.R. Robert Capa  *Magnum, Ladies' Home Journal*

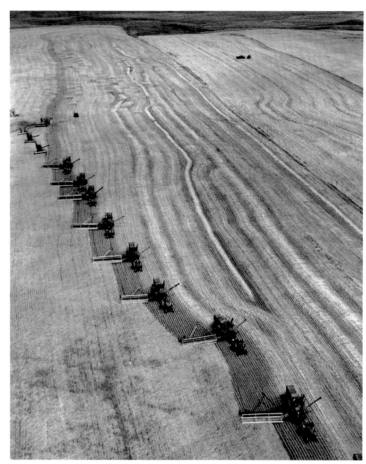

U.S.A. Loomis Dean  *Life*

U.S.A. Edward Clark  *Life*

U.S.A. Jack Delano  *Farm Security Adm.*

Ireland. G. H. Metcalf  *Black Star*

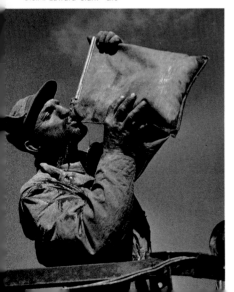

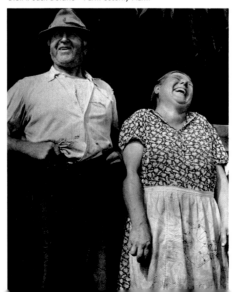

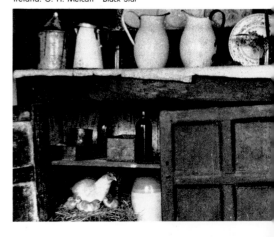

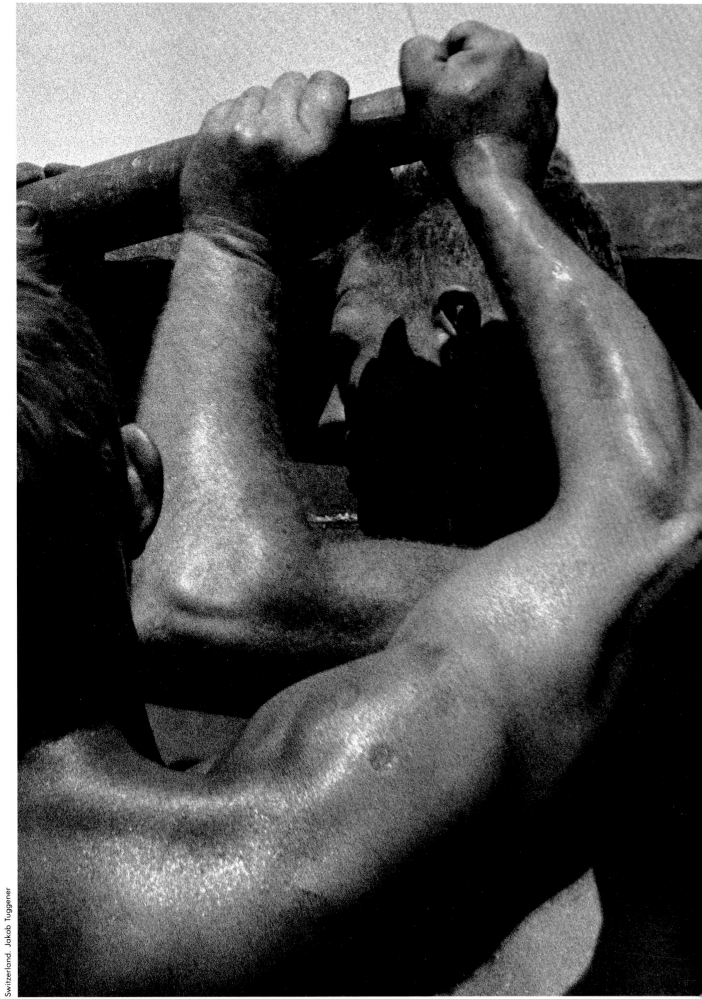

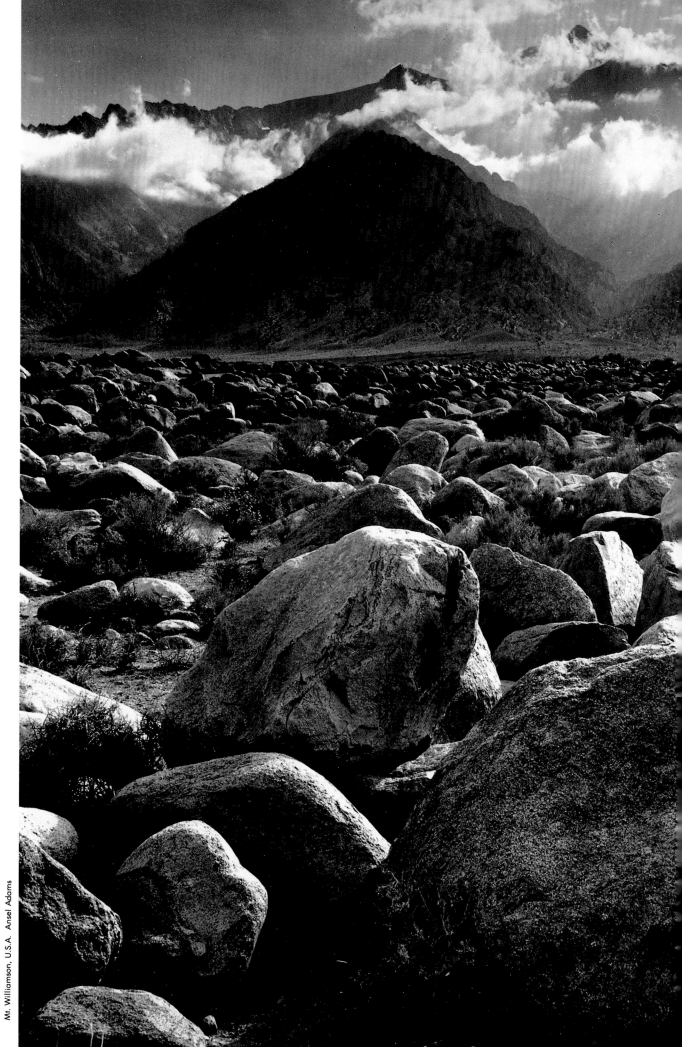

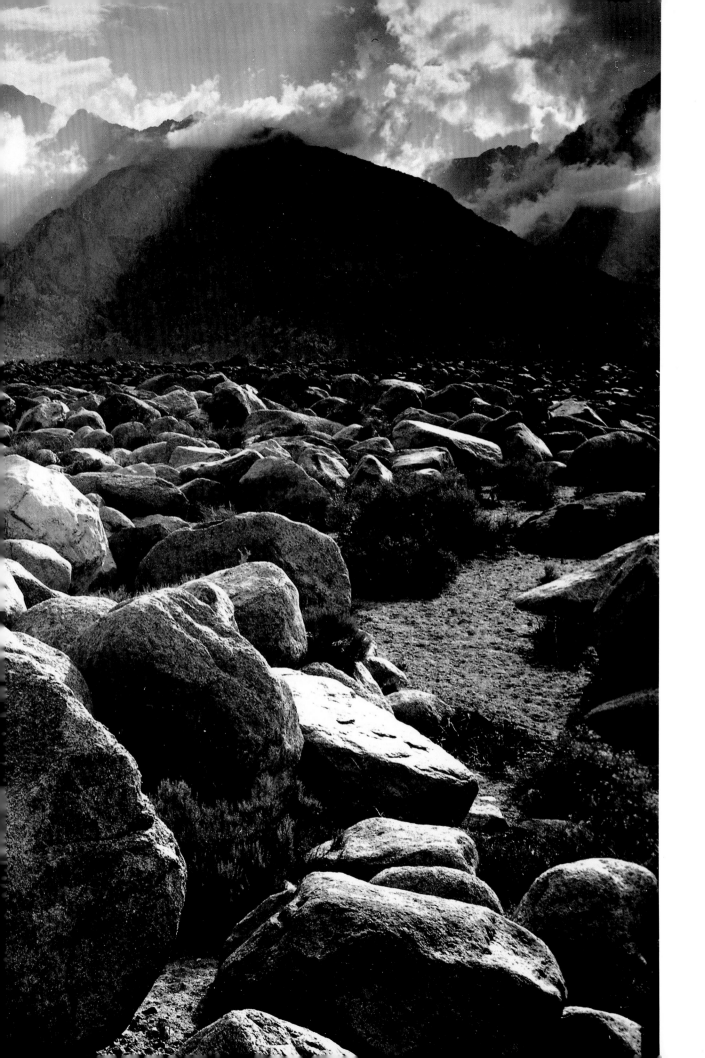

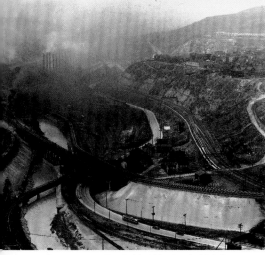

U.S.A. Todd Webb   *Standard Oil of New Jersey*

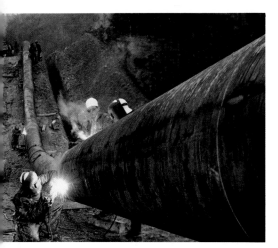

U.S.A. Margaret Bourke-White   *Life*

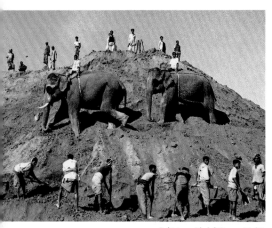

Pakistan. Abdul Razaq Mehta

U.S.A. Charles Rotkin   *PFI, Republic Steel*

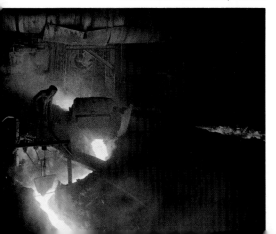

U.S.A. Robert Mottar   *Scope*

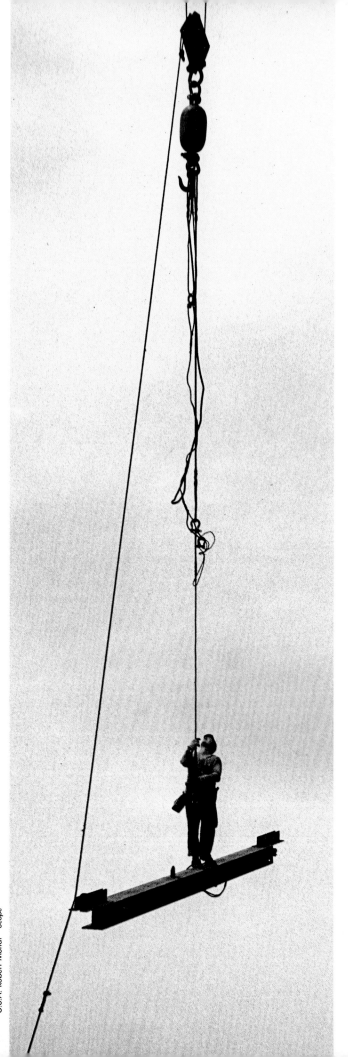

India. Howard Sochurek   *Life*

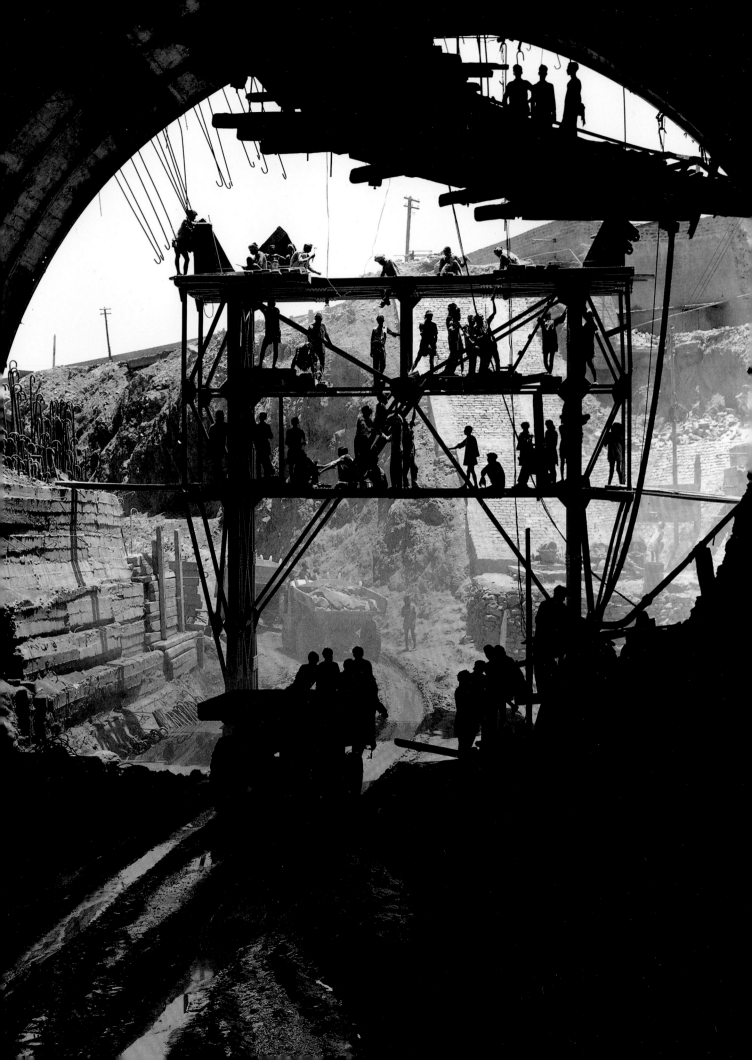

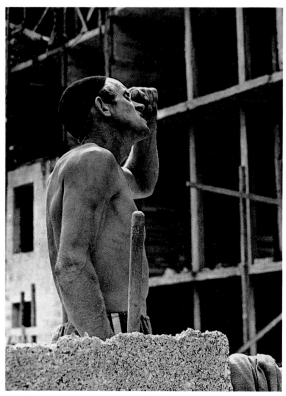

Denmark. Wermund Bendtsen

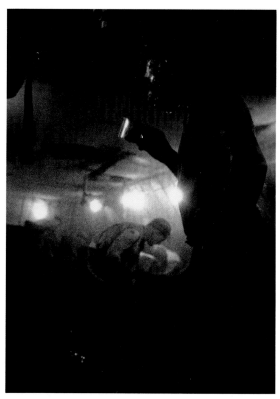

U.S.A. Ernst Haas   *Magnum, Argosy*

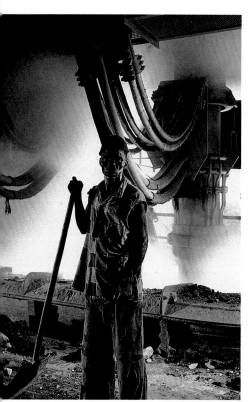

Belgian Congo. Dmitri Kessel

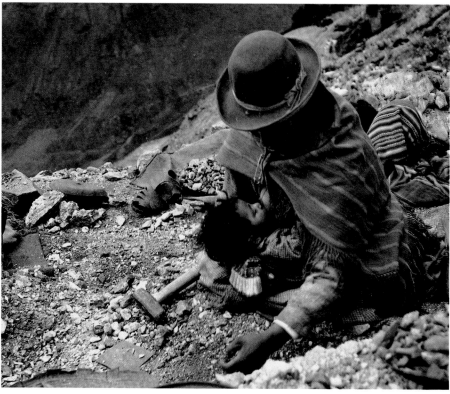

Bolivia. Gustav Thorlichen

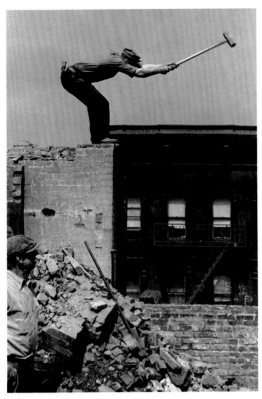

U.S.A. Homer Page  *Argosy*

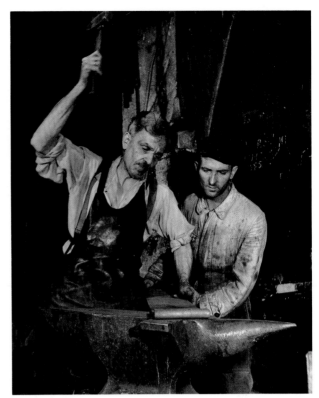

Germany. Walter Sanders  *Life*

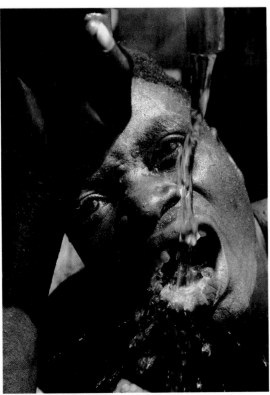

Belgian Congo. Lennart Nilsson  *Black Star*

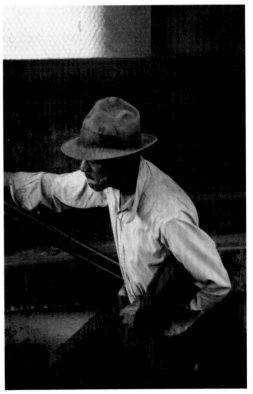

U.S.A. Roy De Carava

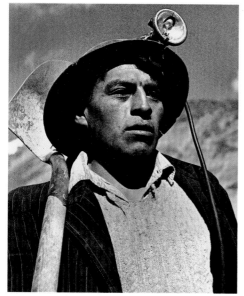

Bolivia. Marcos Chamudes  *Magnum*

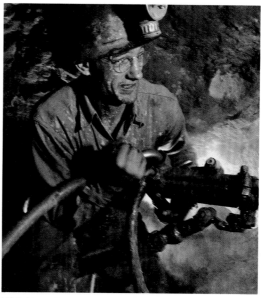

U.S.A. Homer Page  *Argosy*

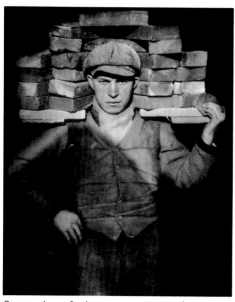

Germany. August Sander

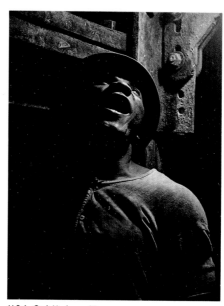

U.S.A. Carl Mydans  *Life*

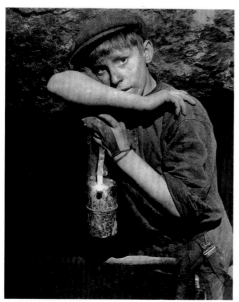

Wales. Frank Scherschel  *Life*

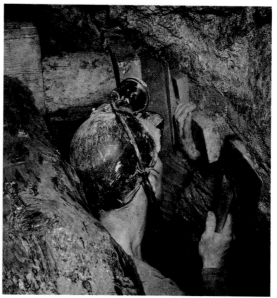

U.S.A. Steinheimer  *Life*

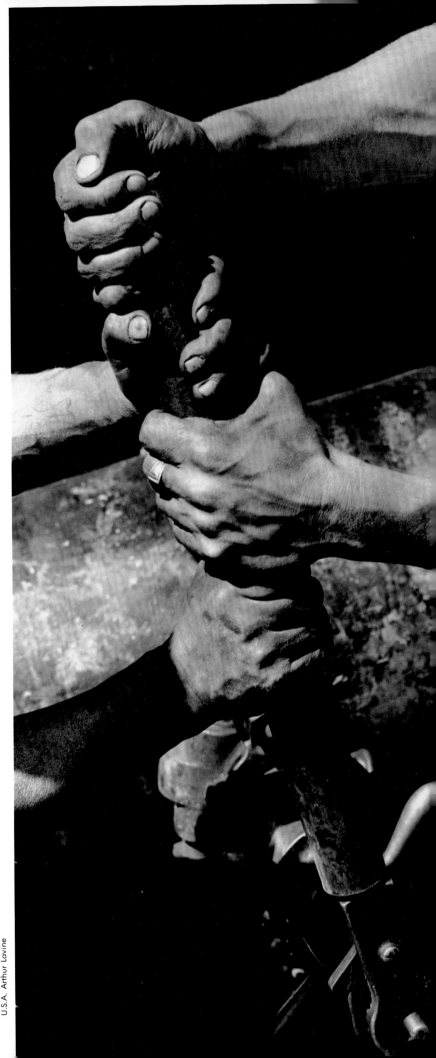

*If I did not work,*

*these worlds would perish . . .*

Bhagavad-Gita

China, Dmitri Kessel  *Life*

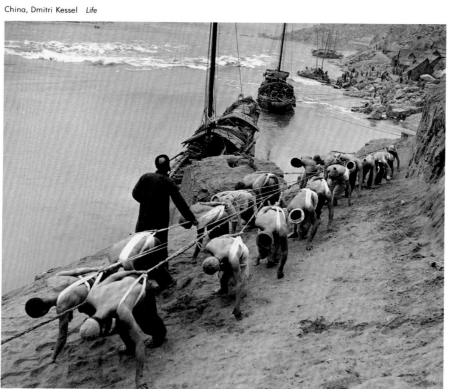

U.S.A. Allan Grant  *Life*

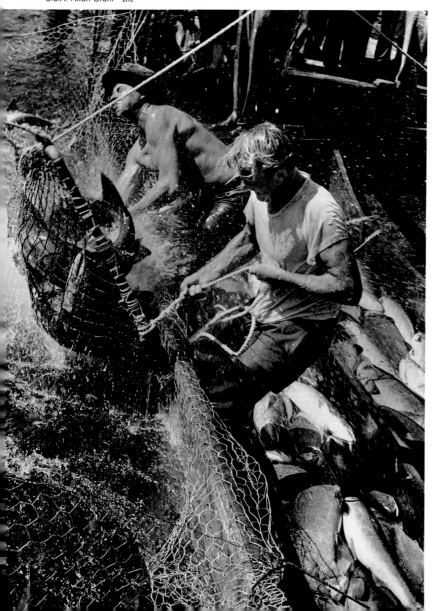

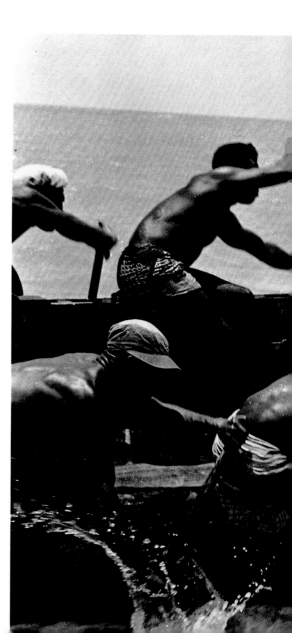

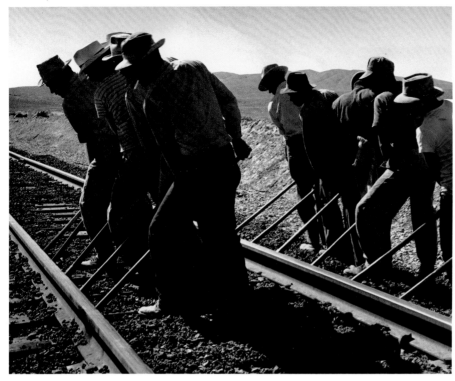

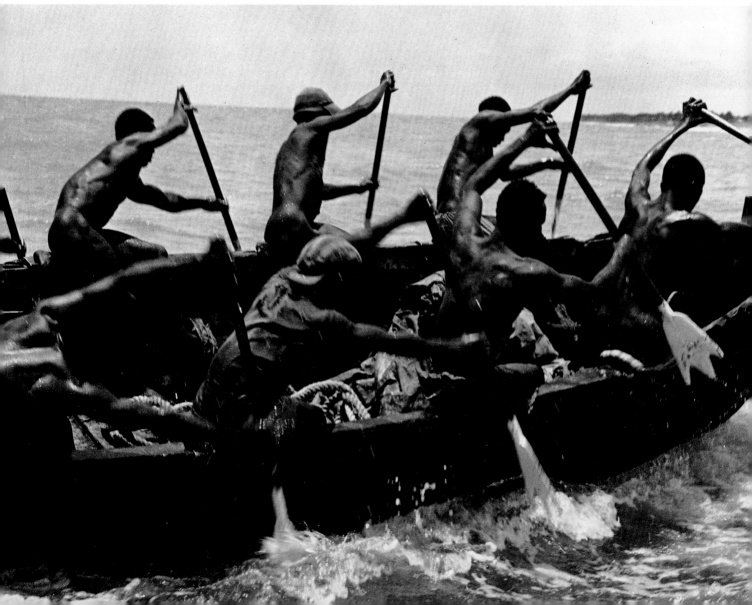

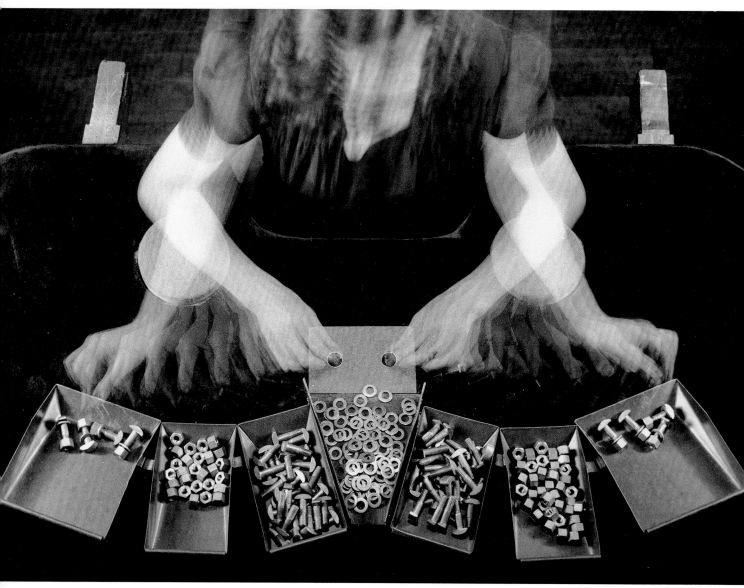

U.S.A. Gjon Mili   *Fortune*

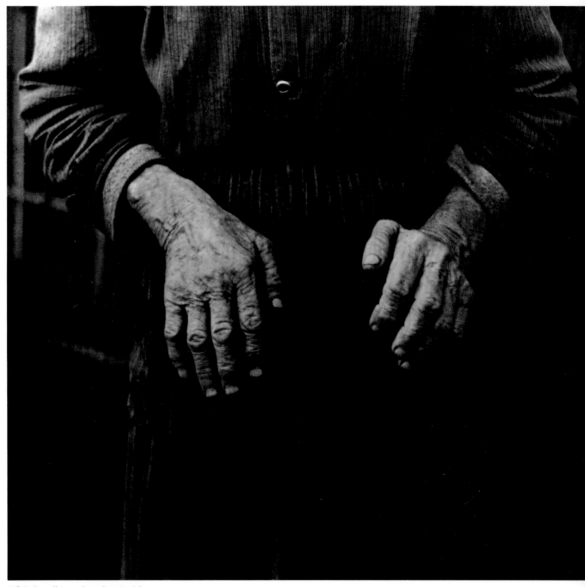

U.S.A. Russell Lee  *Farm Security Adm.*

*Bless thee in all the work of thy hand which thou doest.*

Deuteronomy 14:29

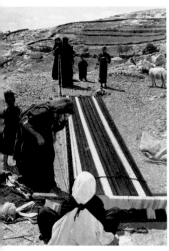

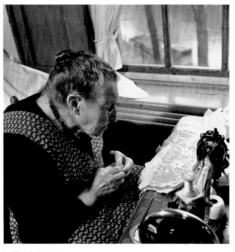

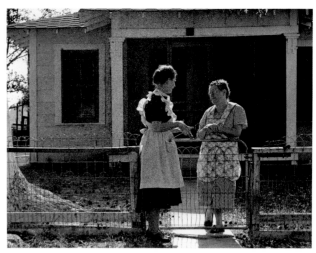

Palestine. David Duncan *Life*          Holland. Eva Besnyo          U.S.A. Simpson Kalisher   *Scope, The Texas Co.*

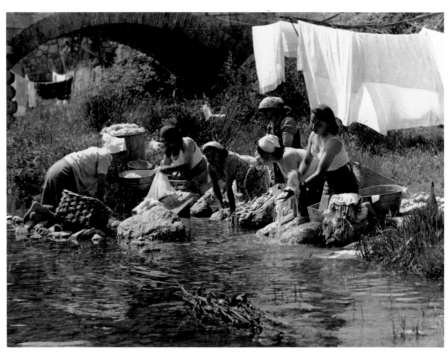

Austria. Emil Obrovsky

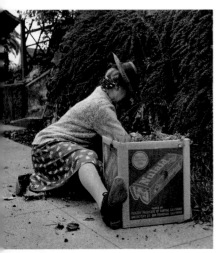

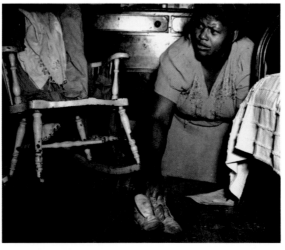

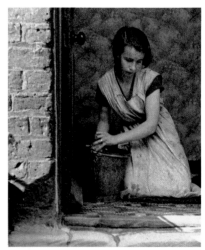

U.S.A. Dorothea Lange          U.S.A. Barbara Morgan          England. Bill Brandt

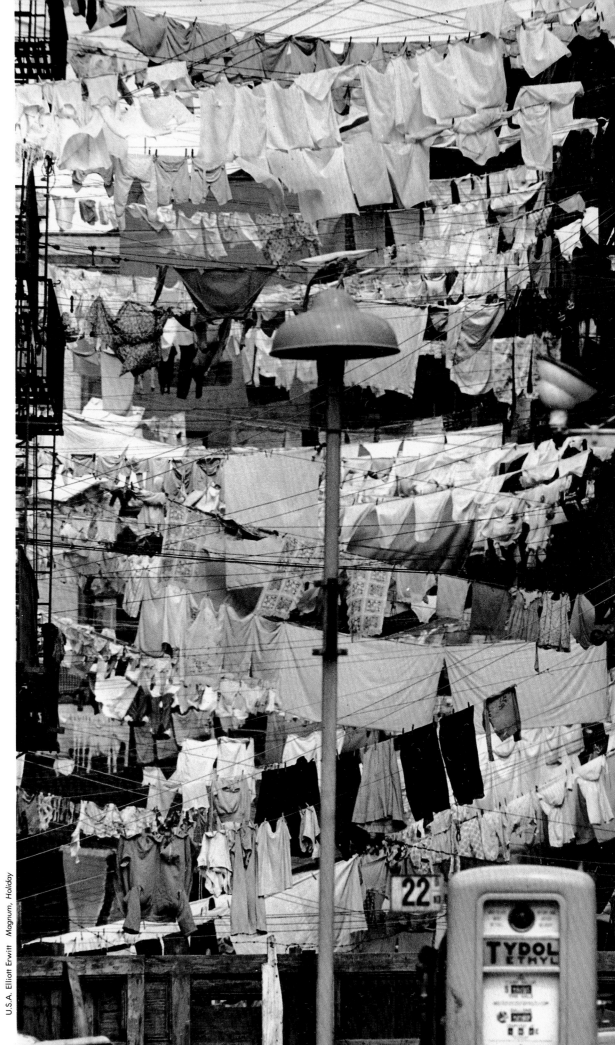

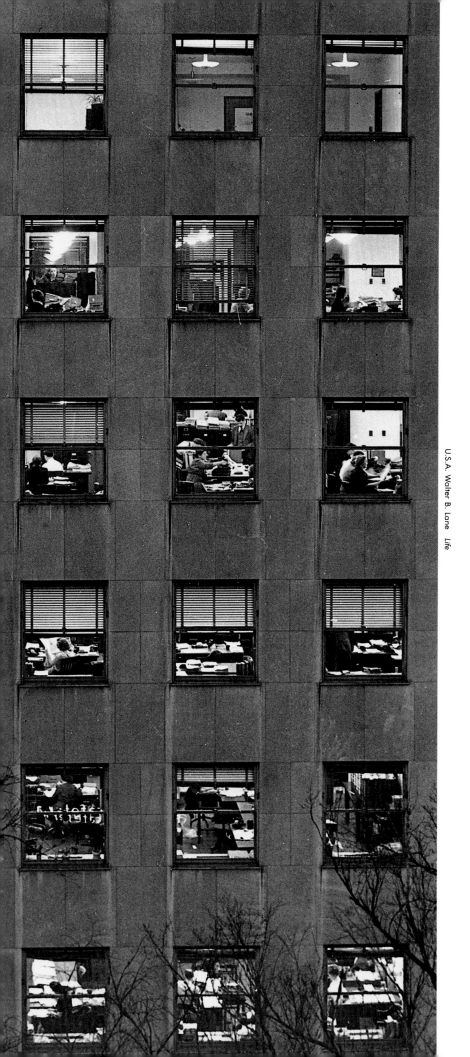

*This is the fire that will*

*help the generations to come,*

*if they use it in a sacred*

*manner. But if they do*

*not use it well, the fire*

*will have the power to*

*do them great harm.*

Sioux Indian

*Nuclear weapons and*

*atomic electric power are*

*symbolic of the atomic age:*

*On one side, frustration*

*and world destruction:*

*on the other, creativity*

*and a common ground*

*for peace and cooperation.*

U.S. Atomic Energy Commission

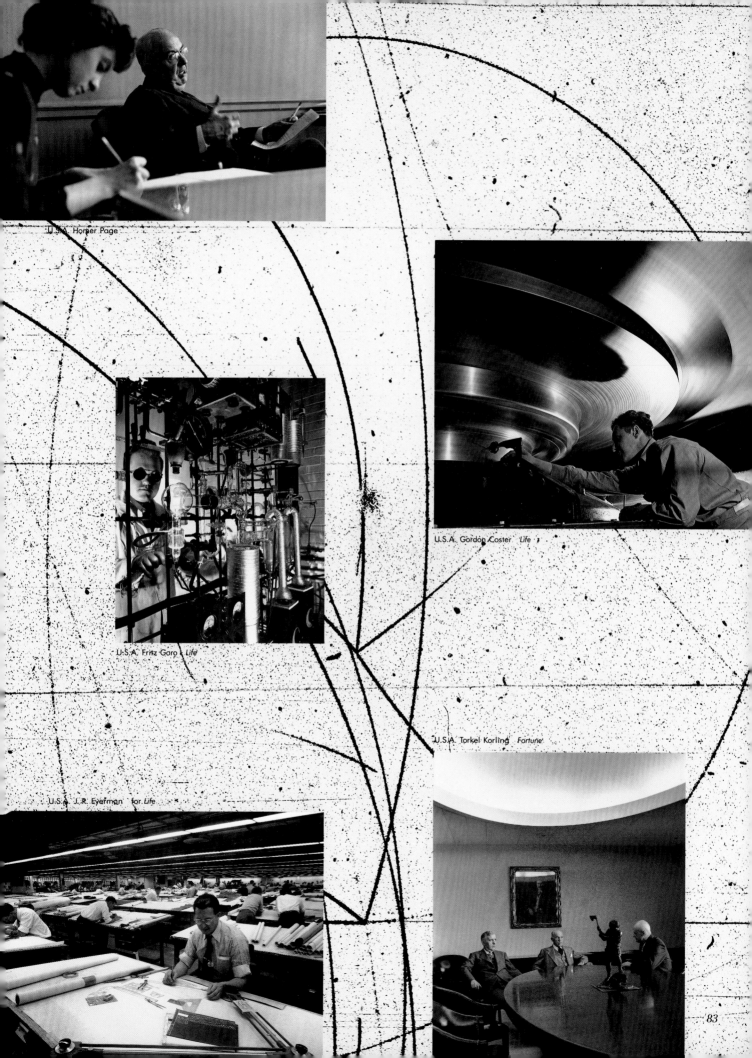

U.S.A. Homer Page

U.S.A. Gordon Coster Life

U.S.A. Fritz Goro Life

U.S.A. Torkel Korling Fortune

U.S.A. J. R. Eyerman for Life

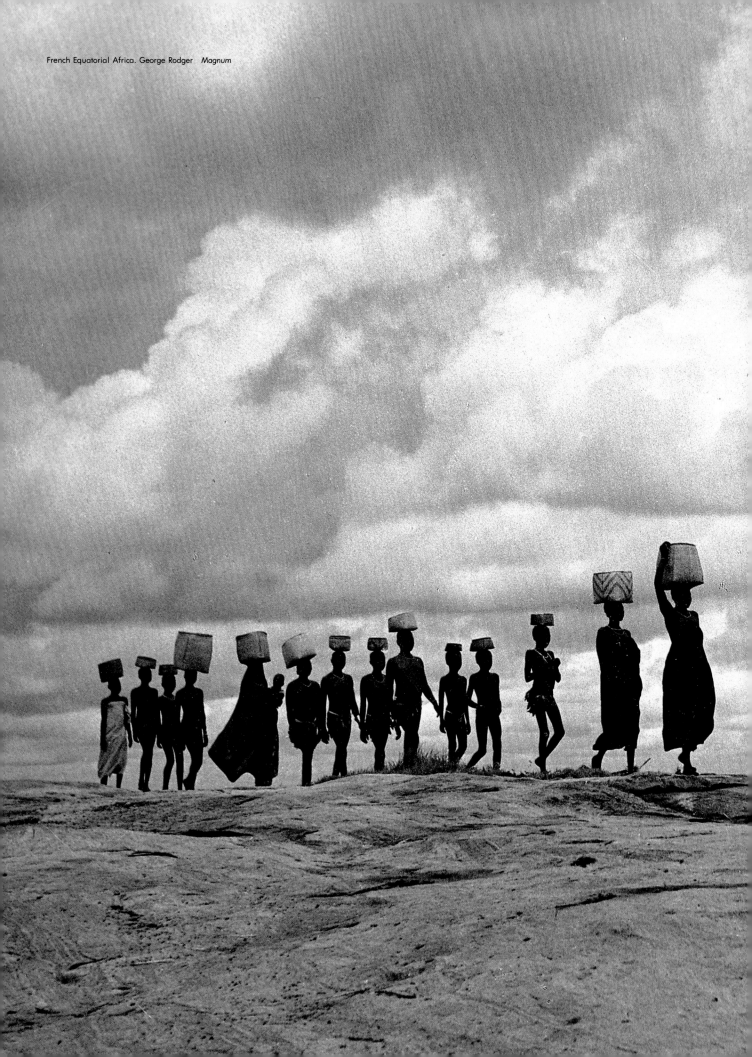

French Equatorial Africa. George Rodger  *Magnum*

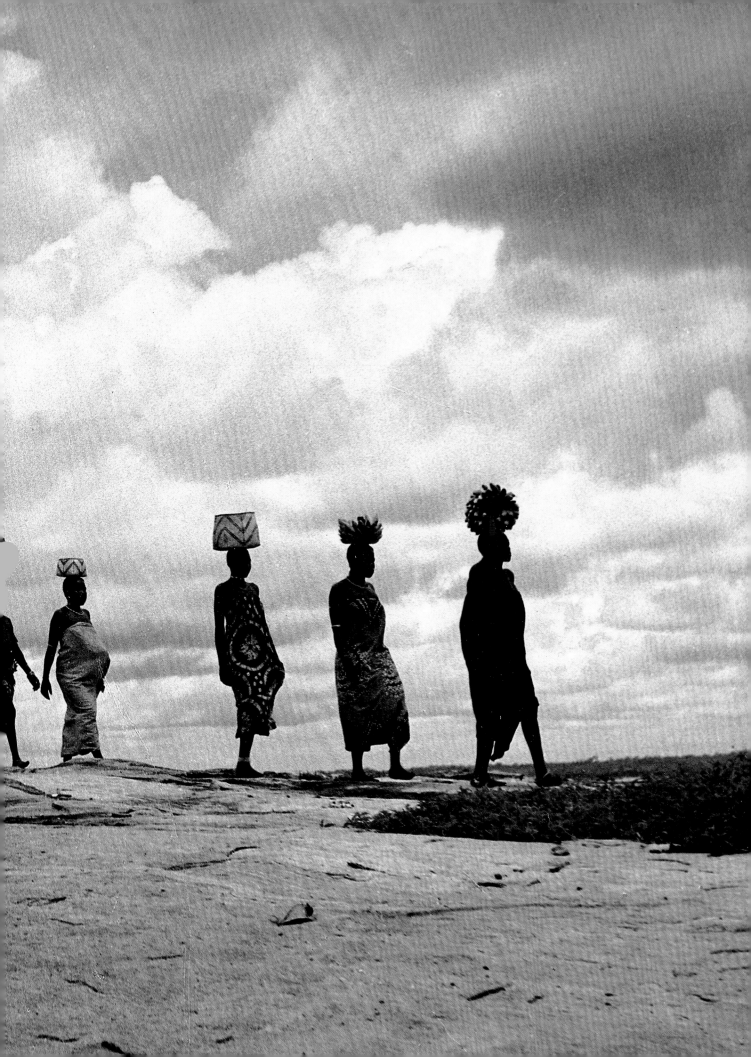

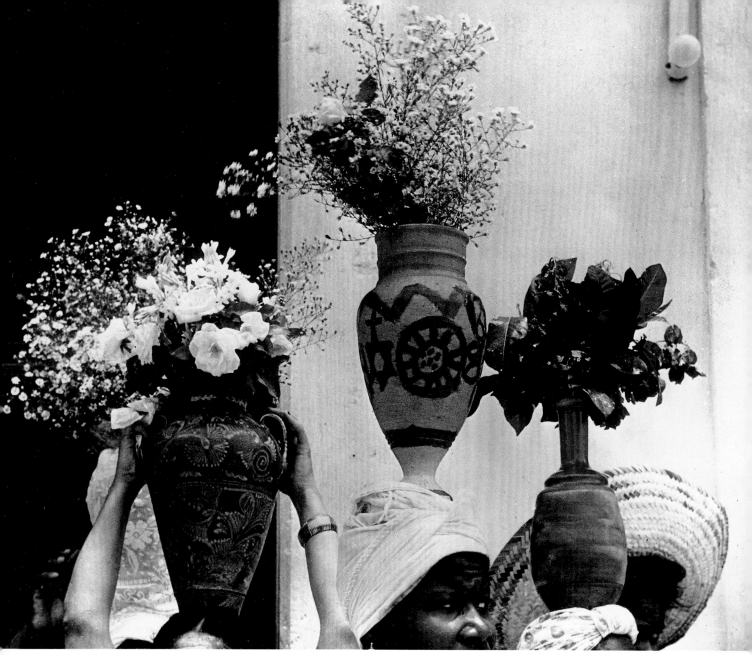

Peru. Pierre Verger  *Adep*

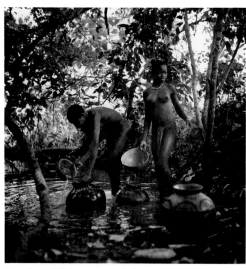

Ivory Coast. Ruth Davis  *Rapho Guillumette*

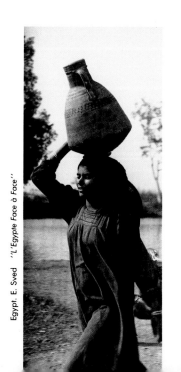

Egypt. E. Sved  *"L'Egypte Face à Face"*

86

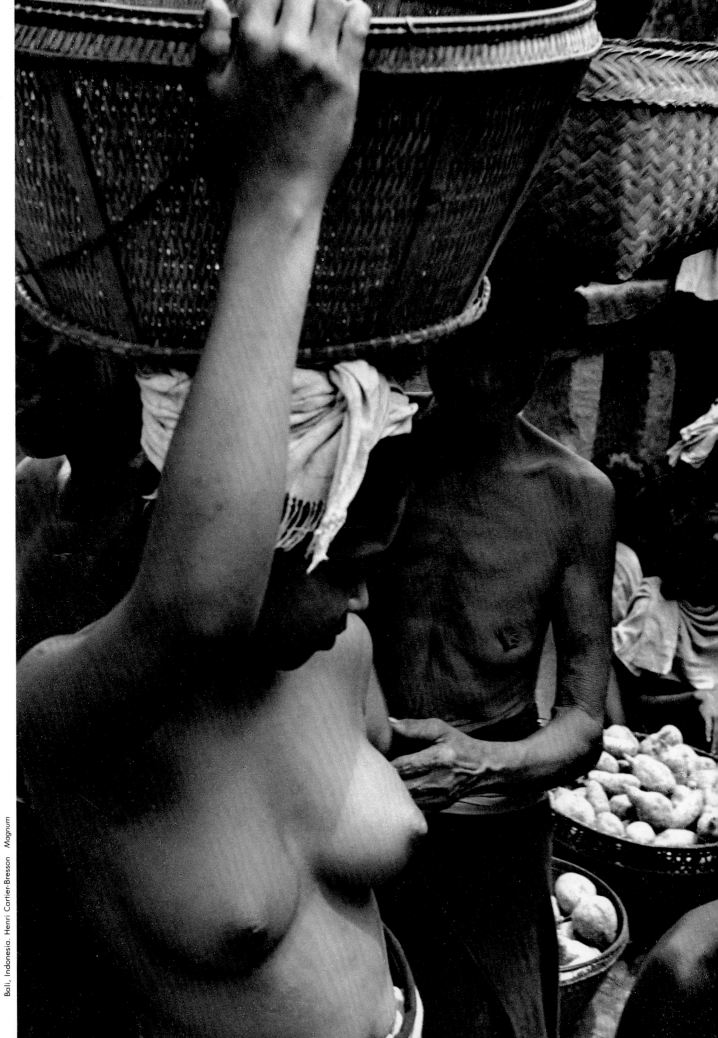

Bali, Indonesia. Henri Cartier-Bresson  *Magnum*

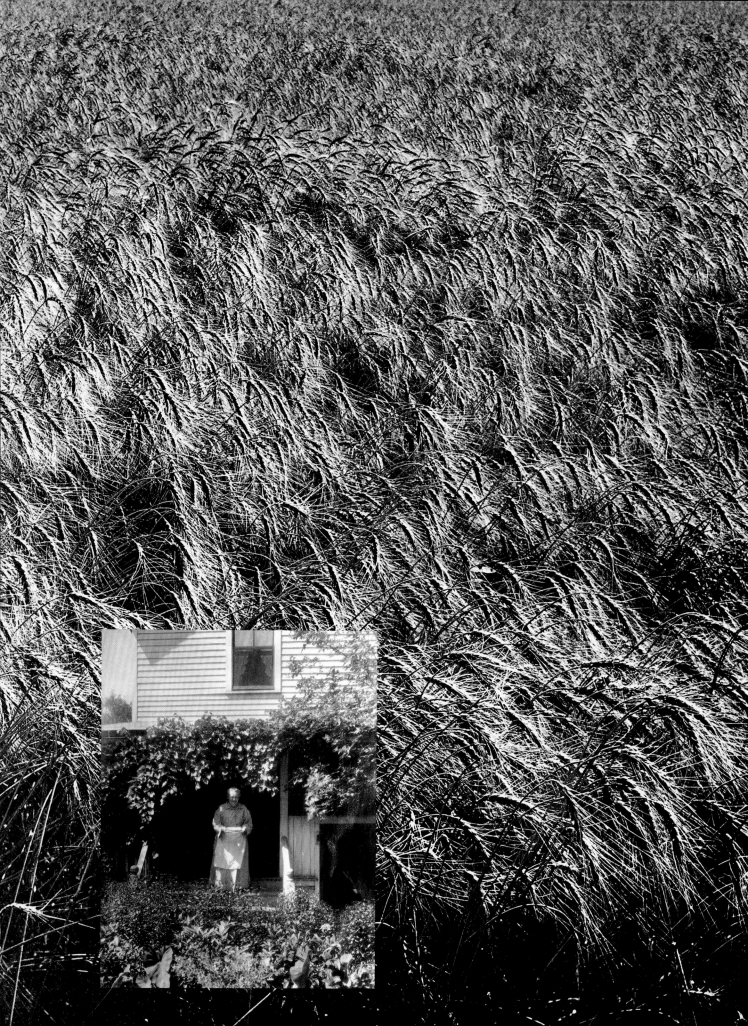

*Eat Bread and Salt and Speak the Truth.*

Russian Proverb

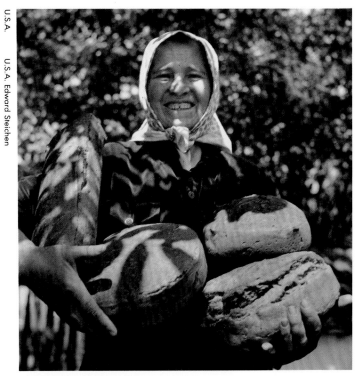

Yugoslavia. Walter Sanders  *Life*

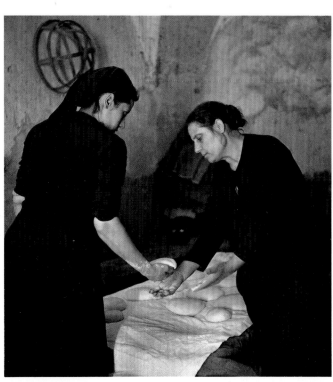

Sicily. Vito Fiorenza

89

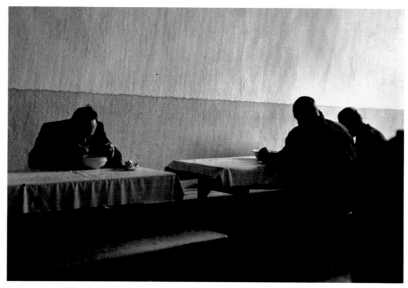

Germany. Rudolf Pollak   *Institut für Bildjournalismus*

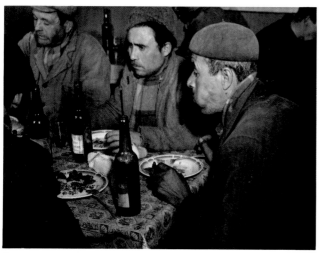

France. Hans A. Schreiner

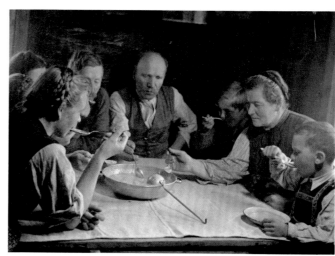

Austria. Leopold Fischer

Belgian Congo. Lennart Nilsson   *Black Star*

France. Henri Cartier-Bresson   *Magnum*

France. Brassaï   *Rapho Guillumette*

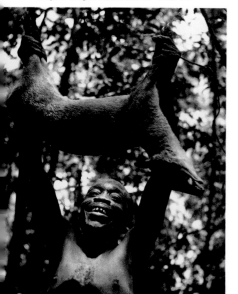

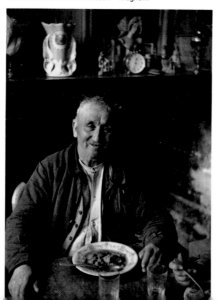

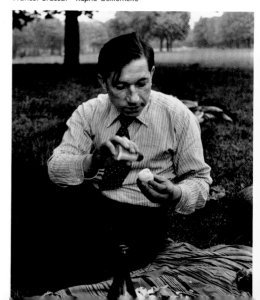

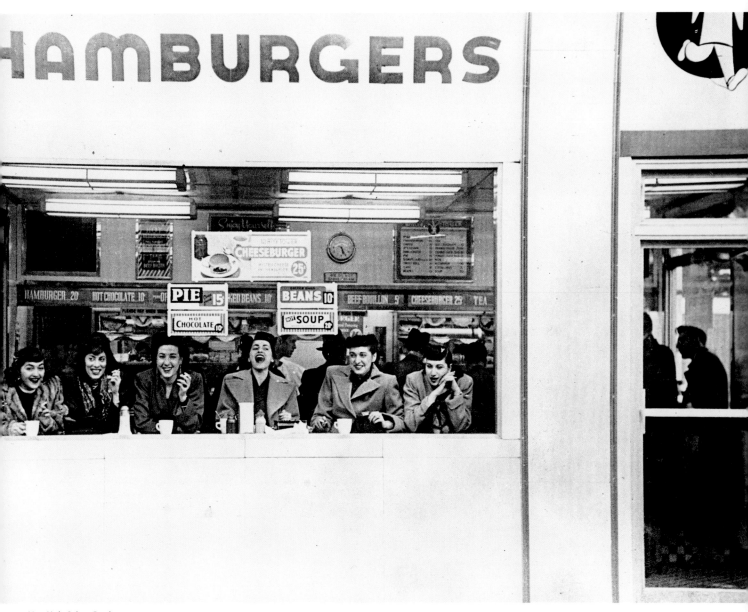

New York. Robert Frank

Japan. Yoshisuke Terao

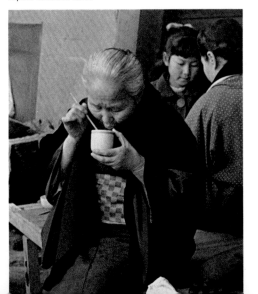

Belgian Congo. Lennart Nilsson  *Black Star*

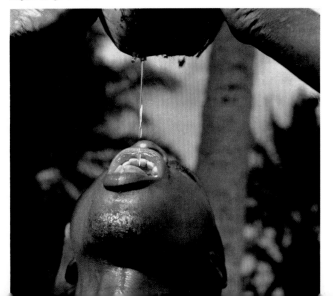

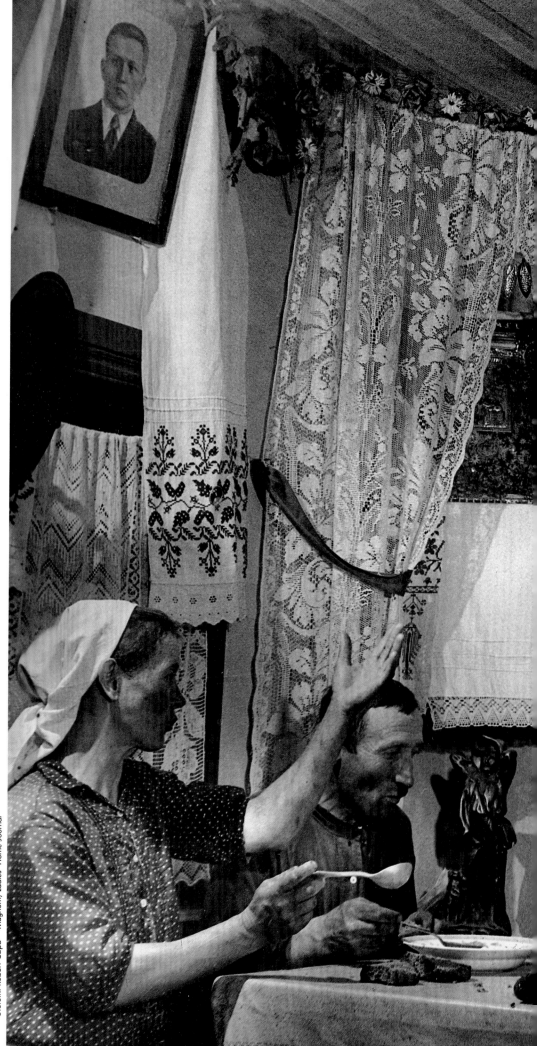

U.S.S.R. Robert Capa    Magnum, Ladies' Home Journal

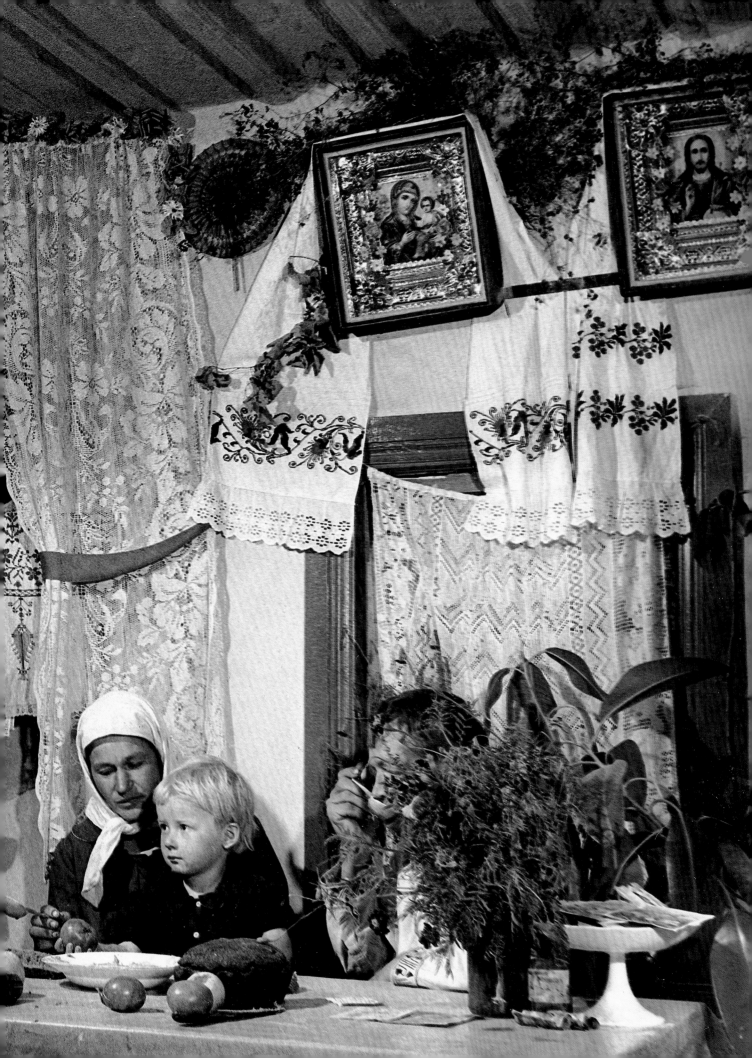

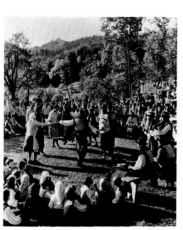

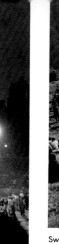

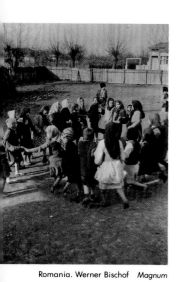

U.S.A. Louis Faurer  *Life*

Switzerland. Ernst Brunner  *Du Magazine*

U.S.S.R., Koslovsky  *Moscow Journalists Club*

Romania. Werner Bischof  *Magnum*

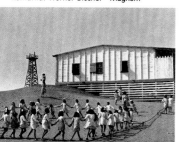

Peru. John Collier  *Standard Oil of New Jersey*

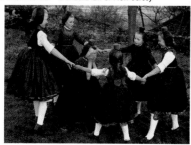

Germany. Erich Andres

*. . .Clasp the hands and know*

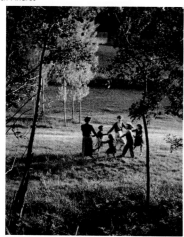

U.S.A. Jerry Cooke  *Life*

France. Vero  *Vue*

Italy. David Seymour  *Magnum, UNESCO*

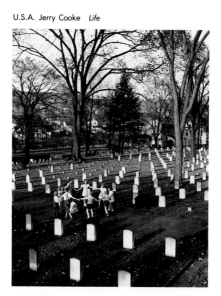

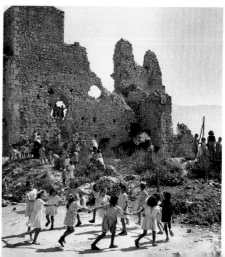

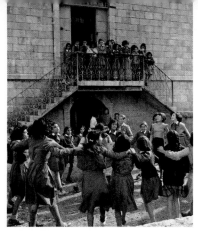

Israel. Robert Capa  *Magnum*

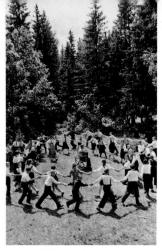

Gorky, U.S.S.R.  *Sovfoto*

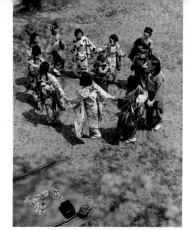

Japan. Hiroshi Hamaya

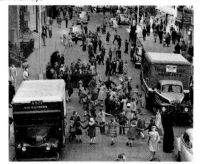

U.S.A. Paul Berg  *St. Louis Post-Dispatch*

*the thoughts of men in other lands . . .*

John Masefield

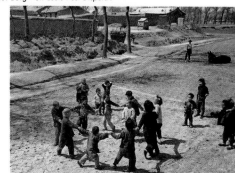

China. Dmitri Kessel  *Life*

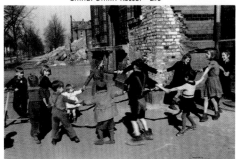

Germany. Hermann Claasen

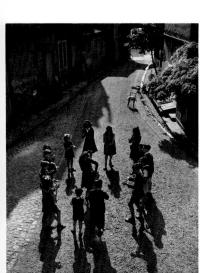

Spain. Ralph Morse  *Life*

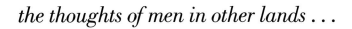

France. François Tuefferd

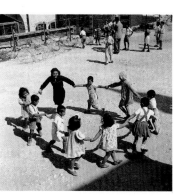

Israel. United Nations

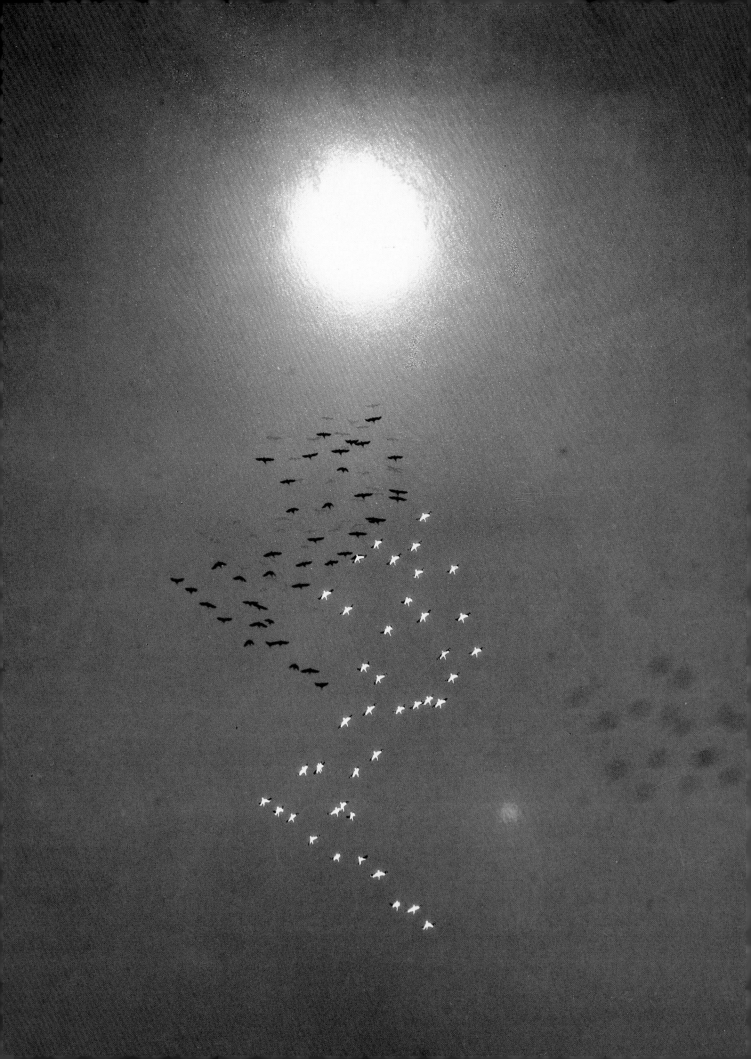

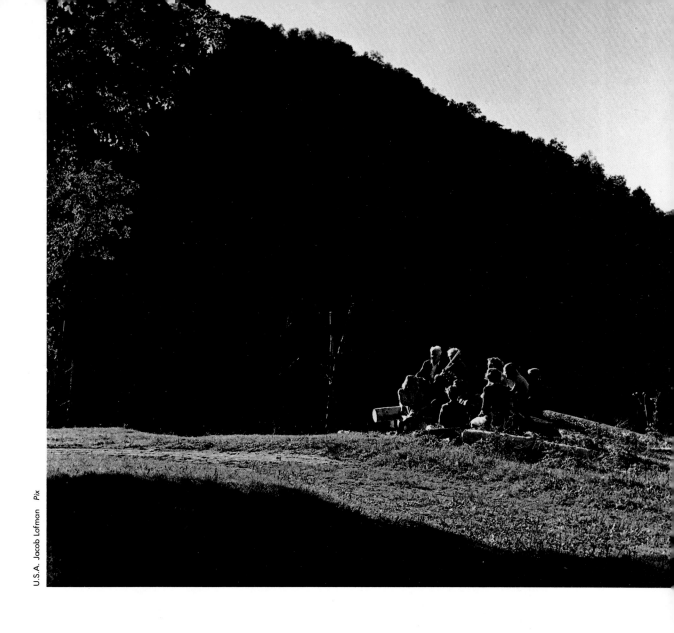

*Sing, sweetness, to the last palpitation of the evening and the breeze*

St.-John Perse

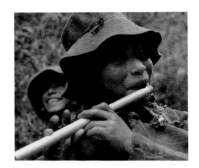

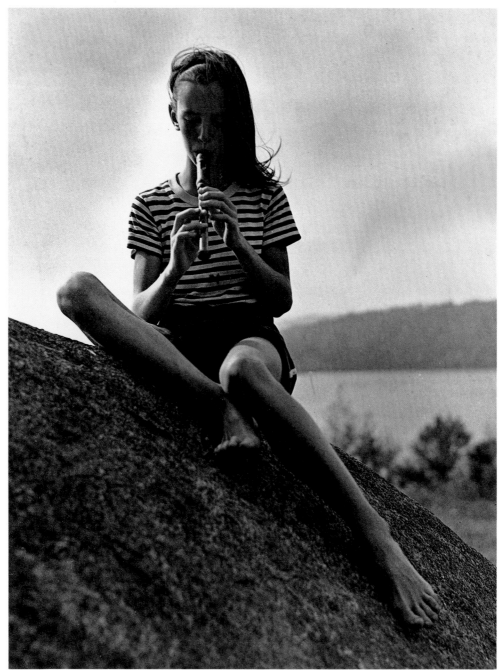

U.S.A. Barbara Morgan

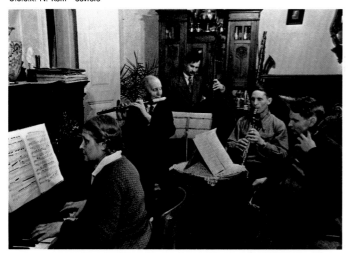

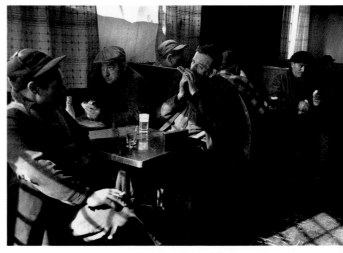

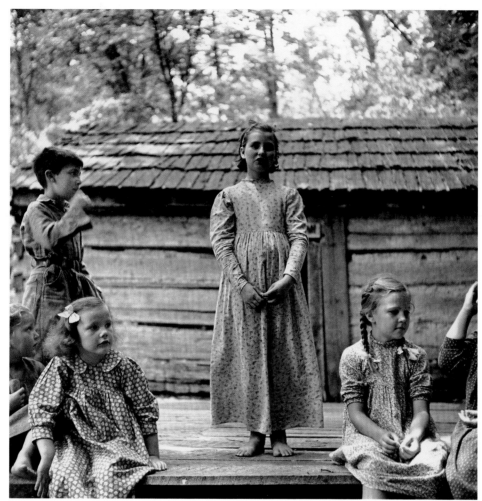

U.S.A. Bradley Smith

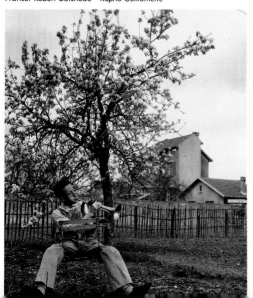

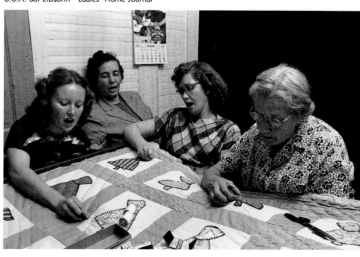

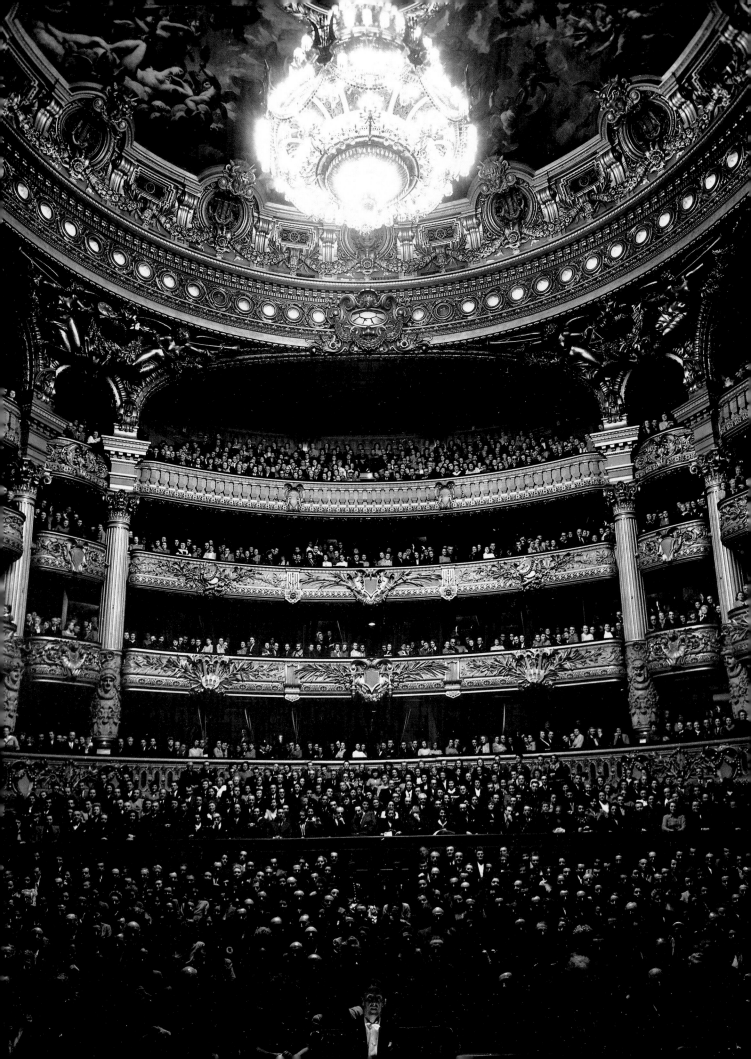

Japan. Werner Bischof *Magnum*

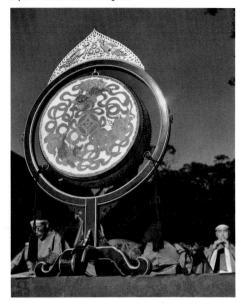

*Music and rhythm find their way into the secret places of the soul.*

Plato

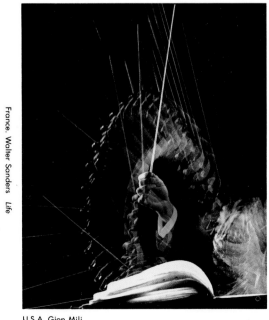

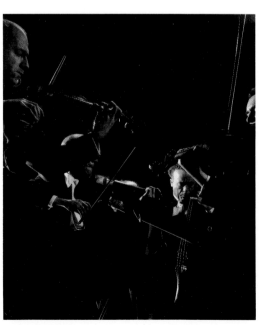

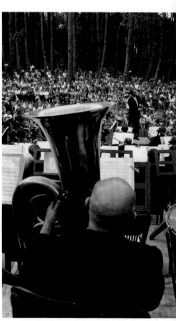

U.S.A. Gjon Mili

U.S.A. Gjon Mili *Life*

Uruguay. Leonard McCombe *Life*

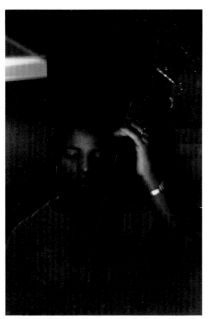

U.S.A. Roy De Carava

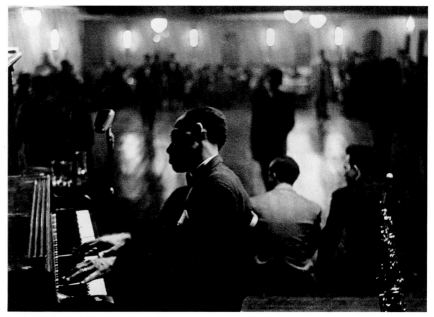

U.S.A. Ed Feingersh  *Pix*

Italy. John Bertolino

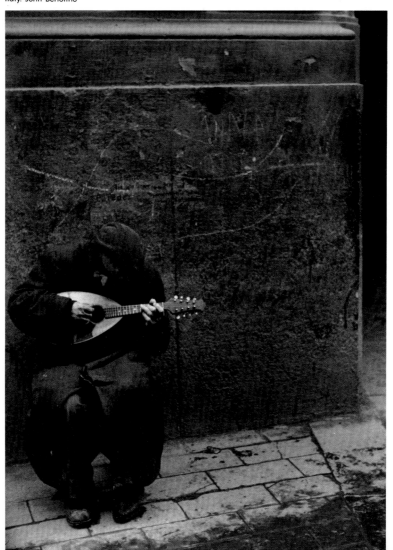

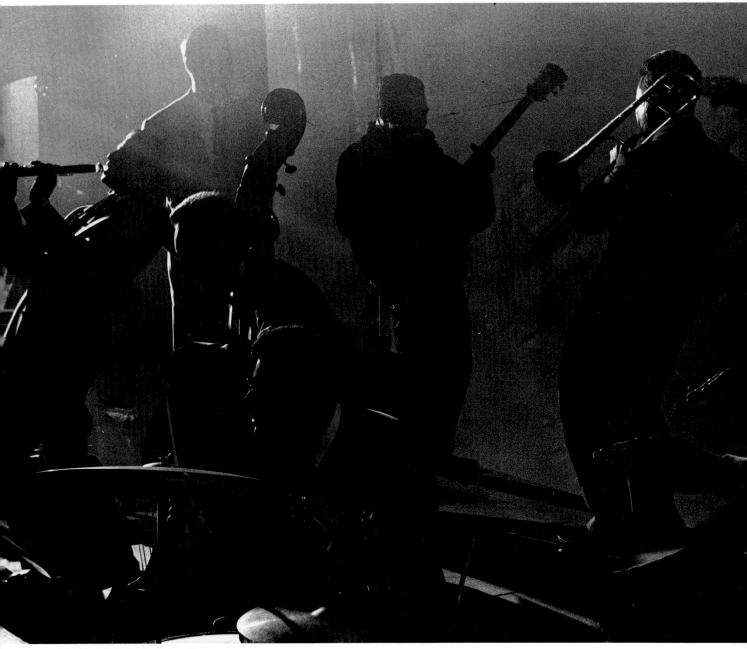

U.S.A. Hugh Bell  *Popular Photography*

U.S.A. Ed Feingersh  *Pix*

U.S.A. Bob Willoughby

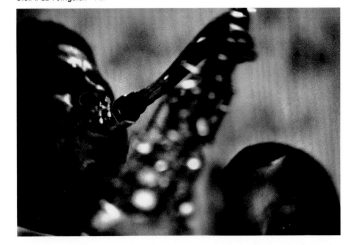

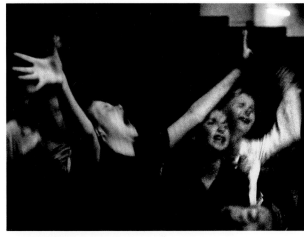

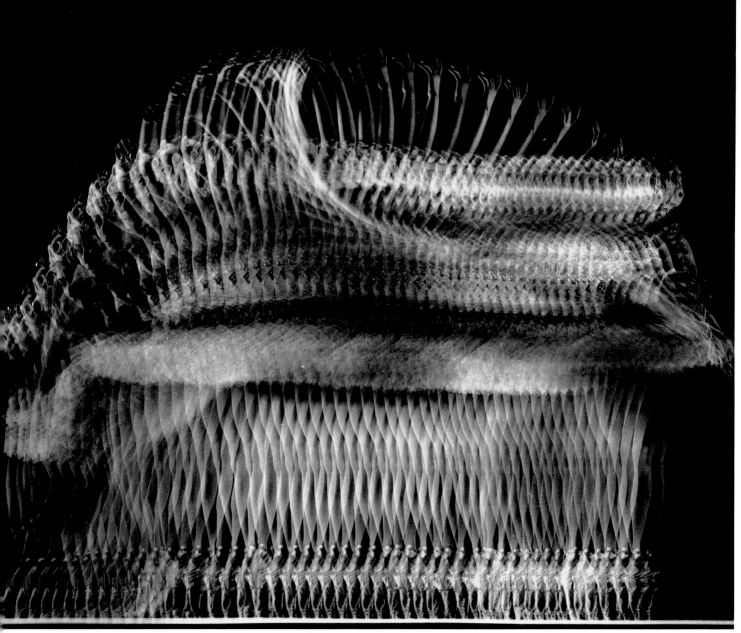

U.S.A. Gjon Mili

*The hills and the sea and the earth dance.*

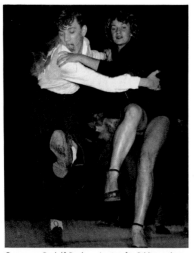

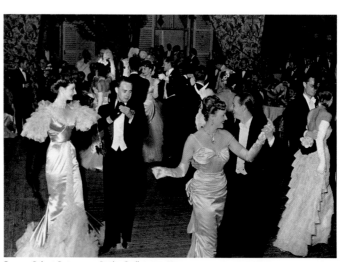

104

Germany. Rudolf Busler   *Institut für Bildjournalismus*

France. Robert Doisneau   *Rapho Guillumette, Vogue*

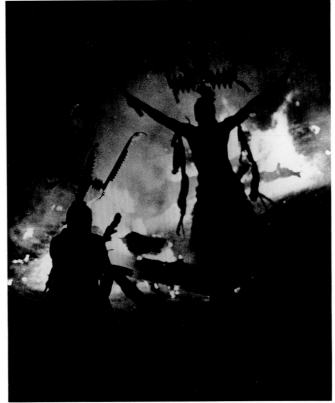

New Mexico. Ernst Haas   *Magnum, Life*

*The world of man dances in laughter and tears.*      Kabir

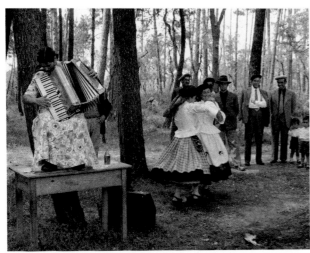

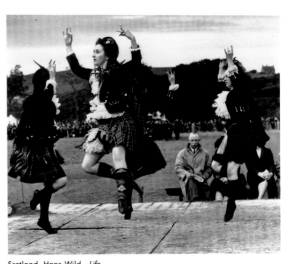

Portugal. Sabine Weiss   *Rapho Guillumette*

Scotland. Hans Wild   *Life*

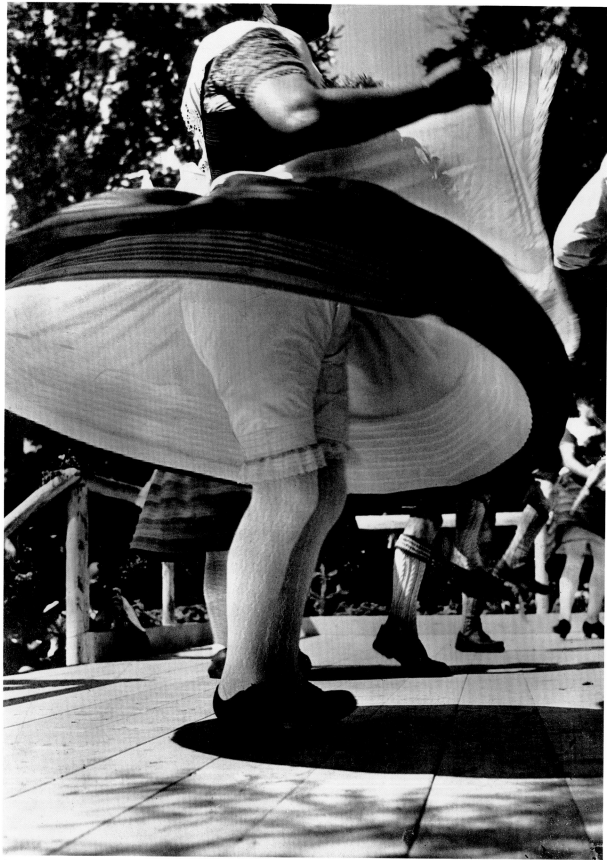

Germany. Kurt Huhle

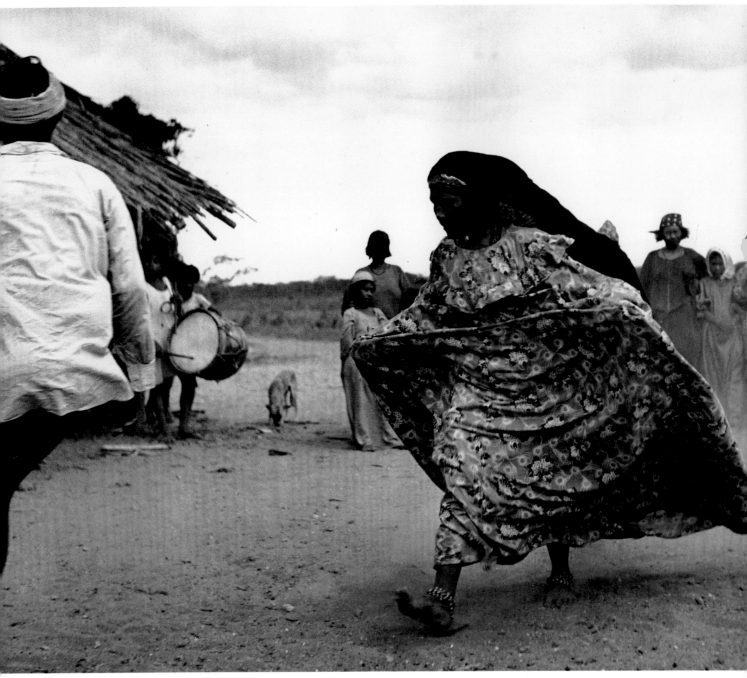

Colombia. Kurt Severin  *Black Star*

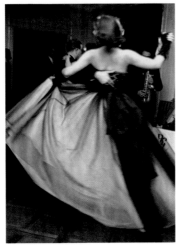

Switzerland. Jakob Tuggener

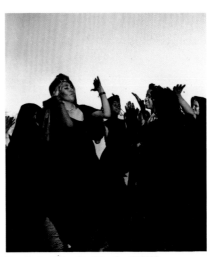

Mauritania, Africa. Eric Schwab  *UNESCO*

107

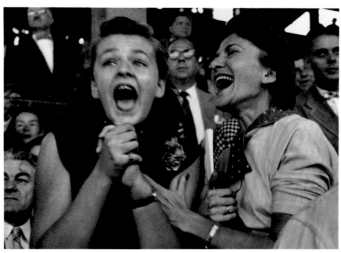

U.S.A. Bob Schwalberg   *Pix*

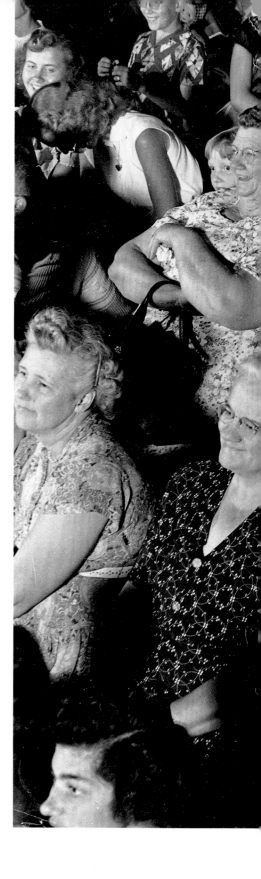

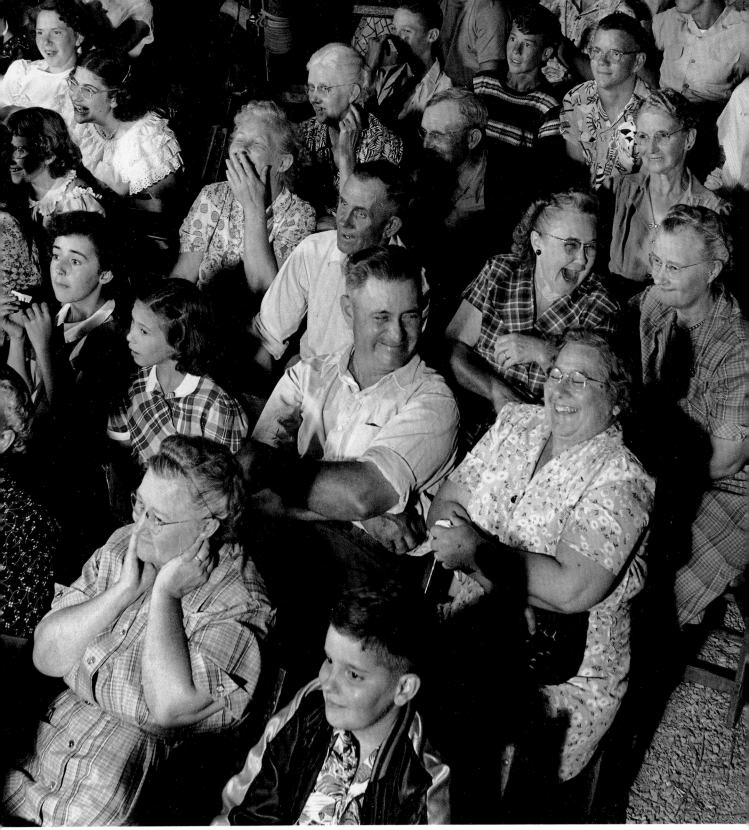

Missouri. Arthur Witmann   *St. Louis Post-Dispatch*

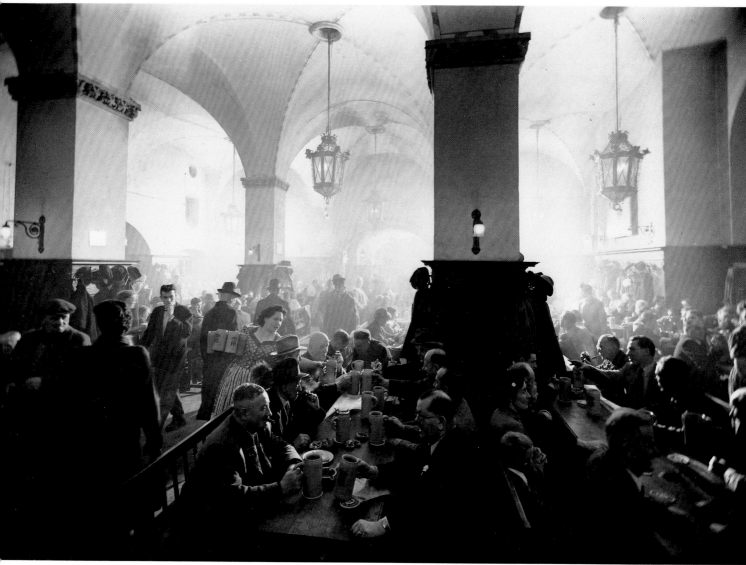

*And the people sat down to eat and to drink, and rose up to play.*     Exodus 32:6

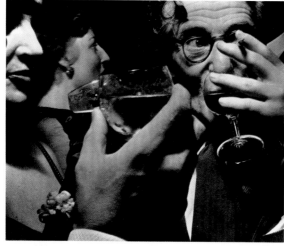

France. Eddy Van der Elsken   *Rapho Guillumette*

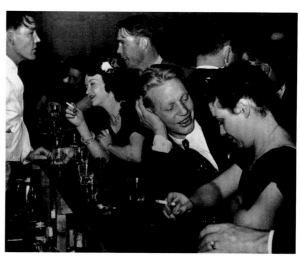

U.S.A. George Strock   *Fortune*

Brazil. Leonti Planskoy

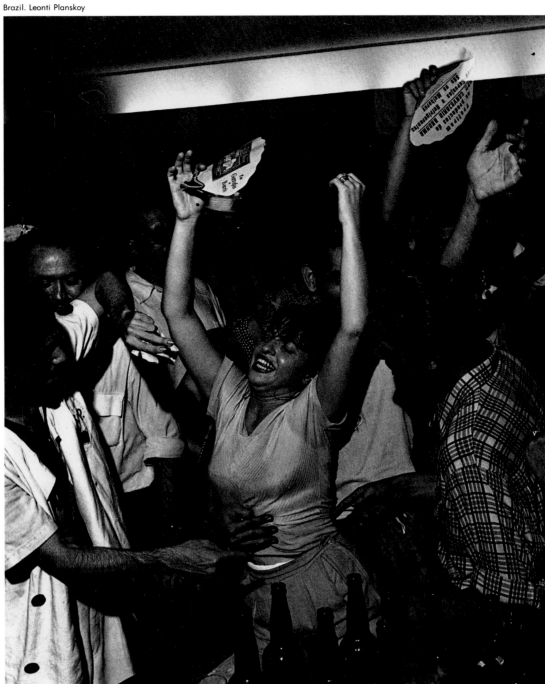

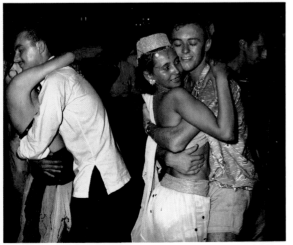

Brazil. Leonti Planskoy

San Francisco. Wayne Miller  *Life*

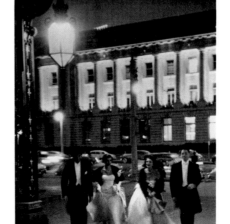

Canada. Ronny Jaques  *Weekend Magazine*

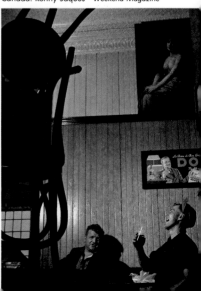

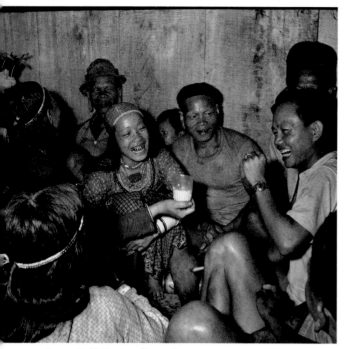

Borneo. Hedda Morrison   *Camera Press*

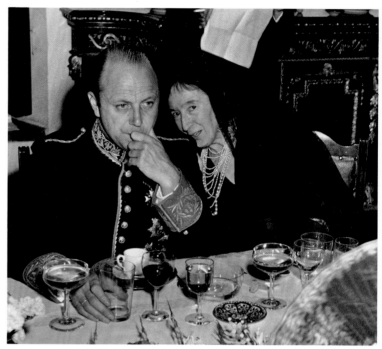

Spain. Frank Scherschel   *Life*

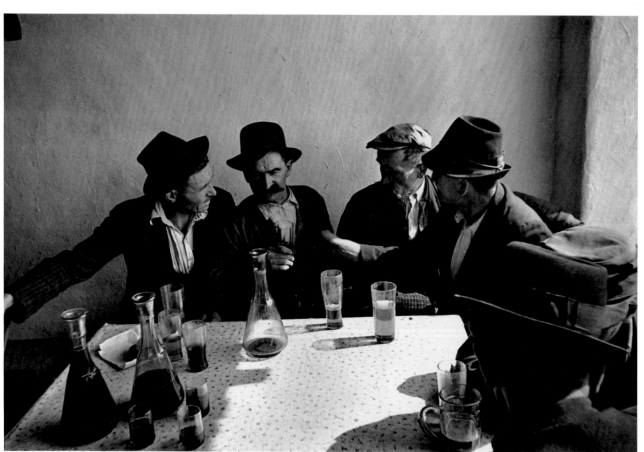

Hungary. Werner Bischof   *Magnum*

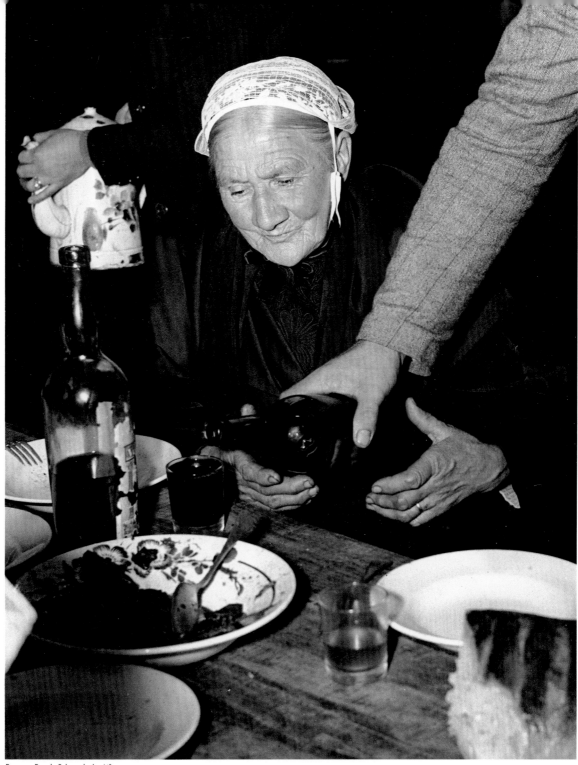

France. Frank Scherschel  *Life*

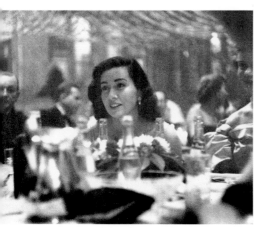

U.S.A. Nick De Morgoli  *Vogue*

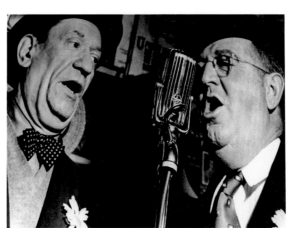

U.S.A. Lisette Model  *Life*

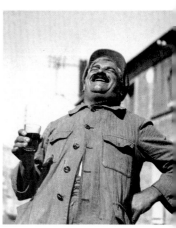

France. Nora Dumas  *Rapho Guillumette*

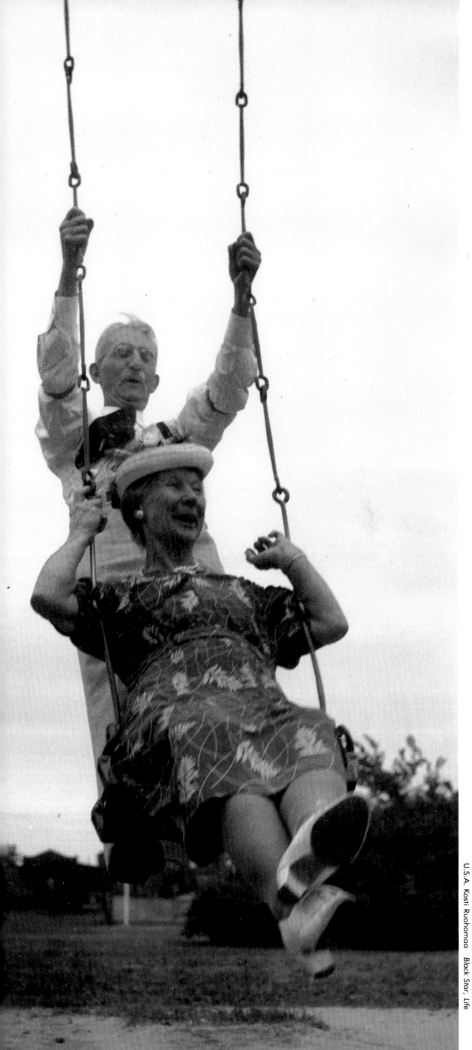

U.S.A. Kosti Ruohomaa  Black Star, Life

France. Brassaï  Rapho Guillumette

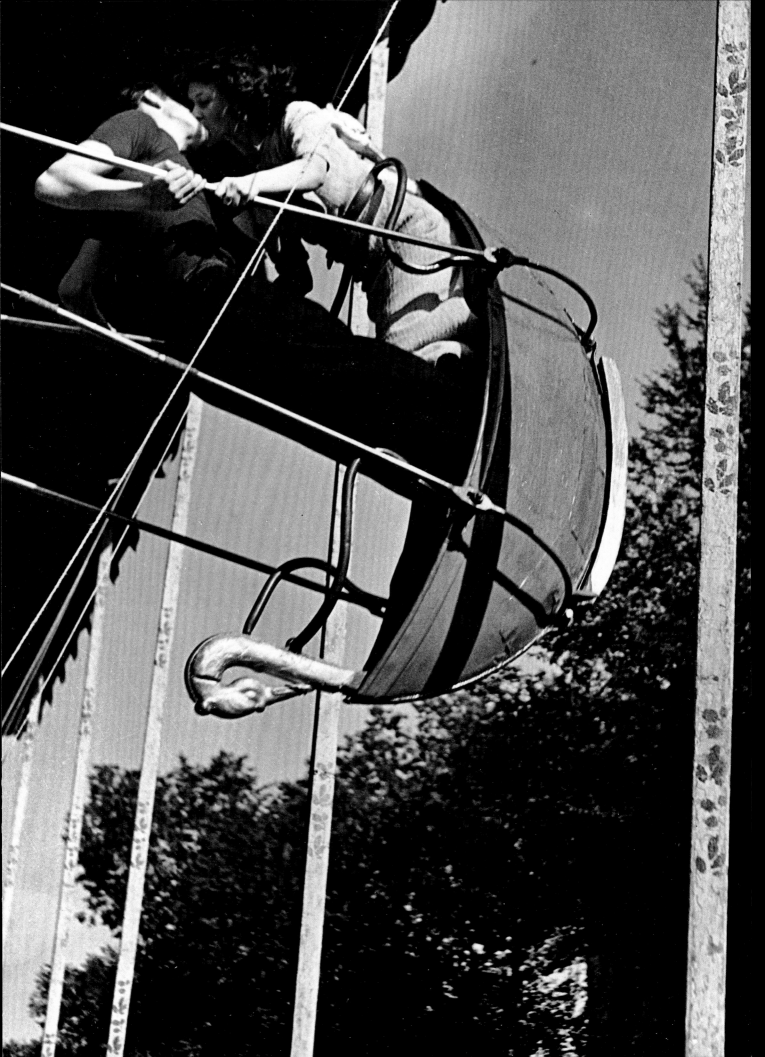

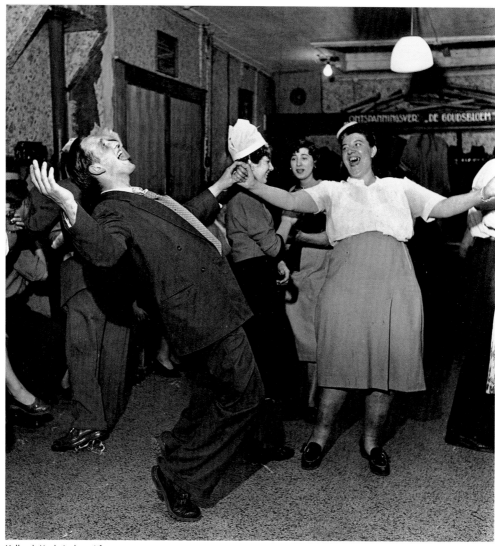

Holland. Henk Jonker  *Life*

Brazil. Leonti Planskoy

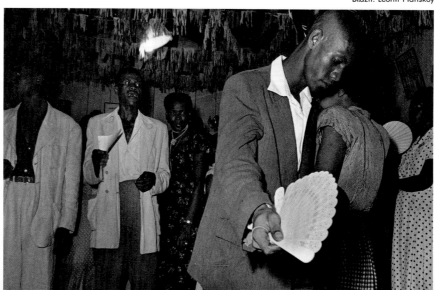

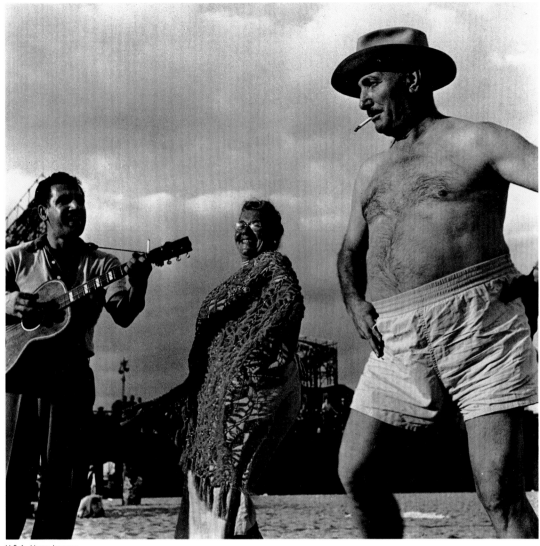

U.S.A. Harry Lapow

Kirghiz Republic. U.S.S.R.  *Sovfoto*

Kirghiz Republic. U.S.S.R.  *Sovfoto*

Sweden. Karl Sandels  *Life*

Canada. David Brooks

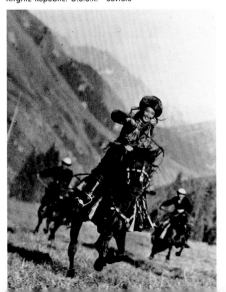

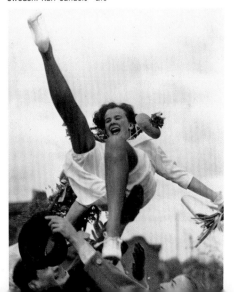

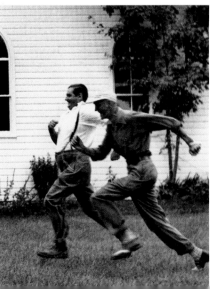

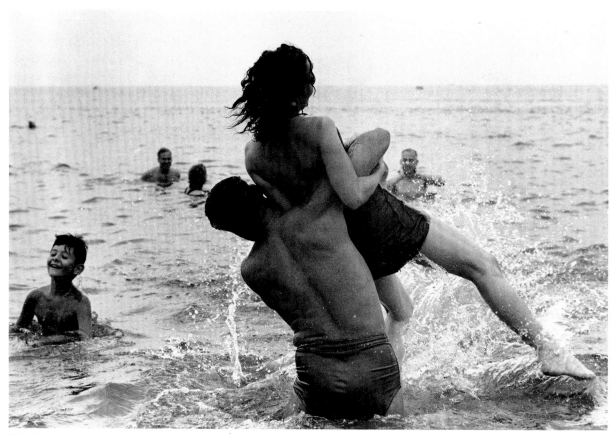

U.S.A. Garry Winogrand  *Brackman Assoc.*

U.S.A. Ewing Krainin  *Life*

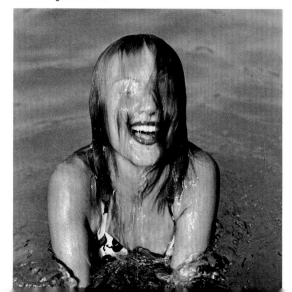

Chicago. Francis Miller  *Life*

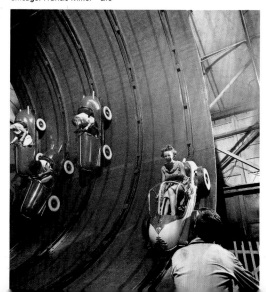

118

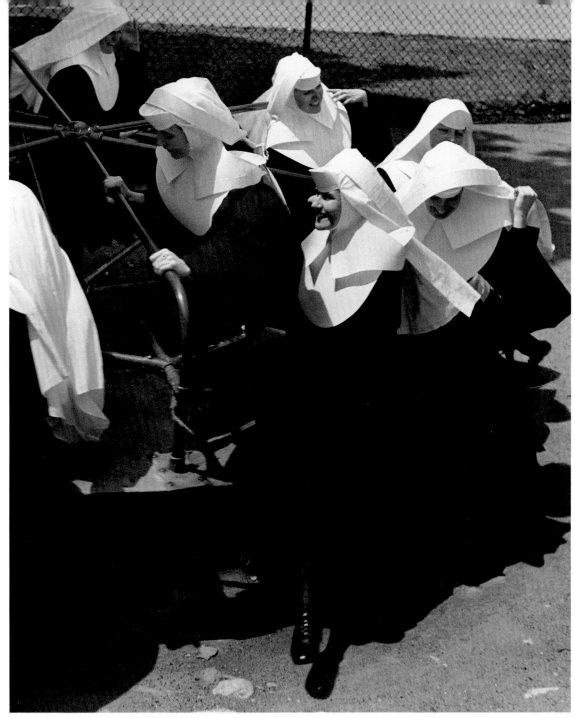

U.S.A. Musya S. Sheeler

Chevy Chase, Md., U.S.A. Edward Clark  *Life*

Jones Beach, U.S.A. Leonard McCombe  *Life*

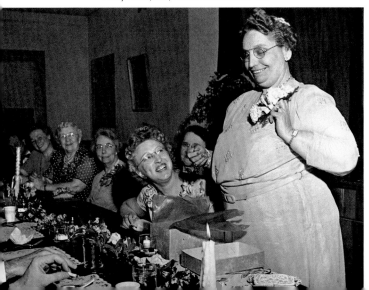

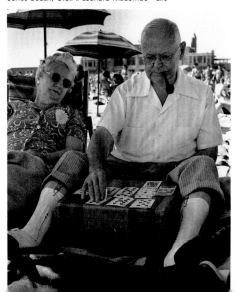

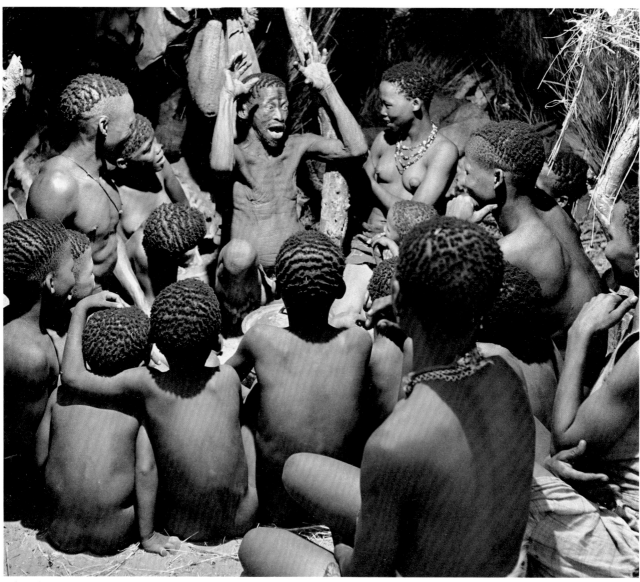

Bechuanaland, Nat Farbman  *Life*

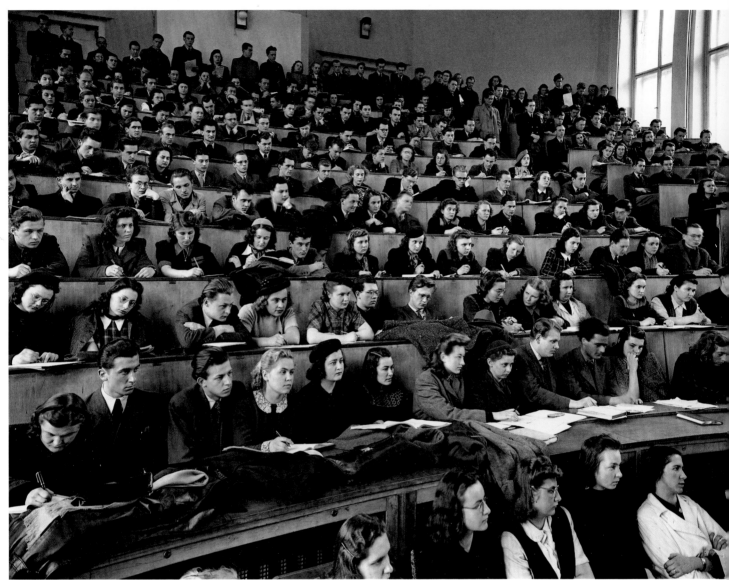

Czechoslovakia. Alfred Eisenstaedt *Life*

*But such is the irresistible nature of truth,*

*that all it asks, and all it wants, is the liberty of appearing.*

Thomas Paine

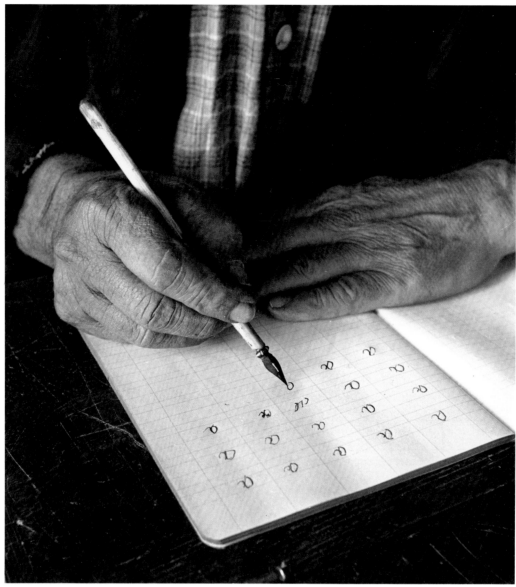

Italy. David Seymour  *Magnum, UNESCO*

Palestine. John Phillips  *Life*

Poland. Roman Vishniac

India. J. De Pietro  *Ladies' Home Journal*

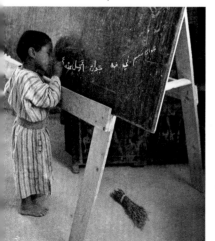

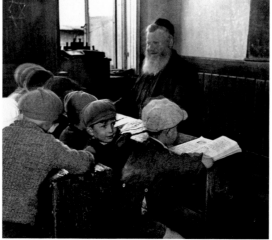

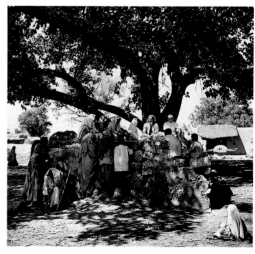

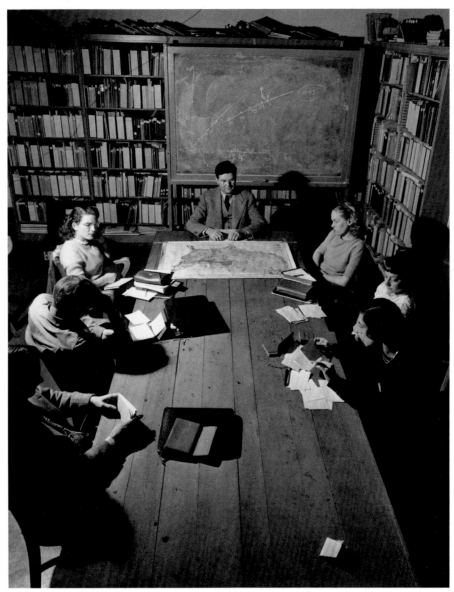

Univ. of California. Otto Hagel  *Fortune*

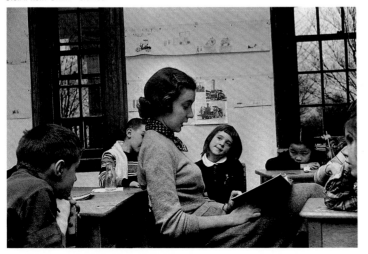

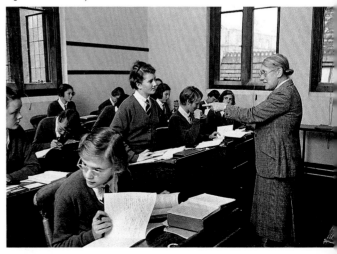

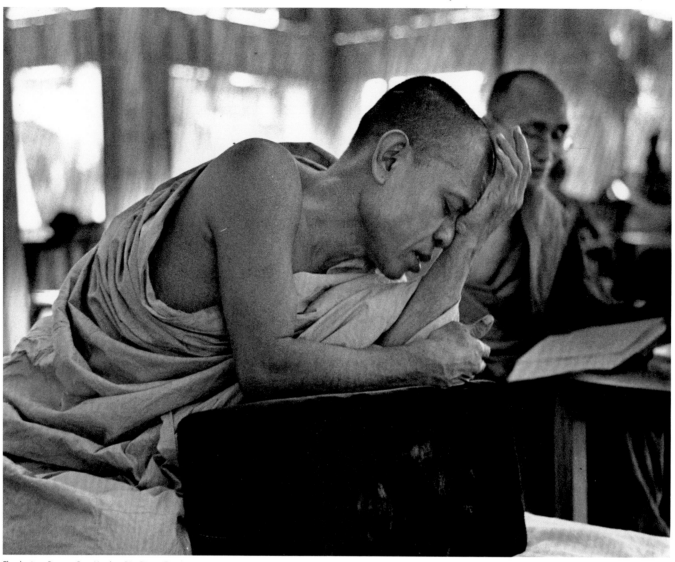

Theologian, Burma. Bert Hardy  *Pix, Picture Post*

*. . . the wise man looks into space,*

*and does not regard the small as too little, nor the great as too big;*

*for he knows that there is no limit to dimensions.*

Lao-tze

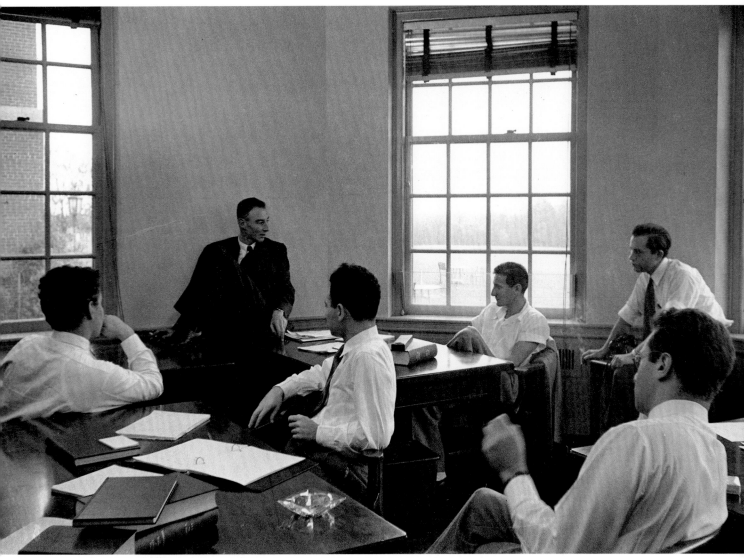

Institute for Advanced Study, Princeton. Eisenstaedt  *Life*

Allentown, Pa. Nina Leen  *Life*

Institute for Advanced Study, Princeton. Ernst Haas  *Magnum, Vogue*

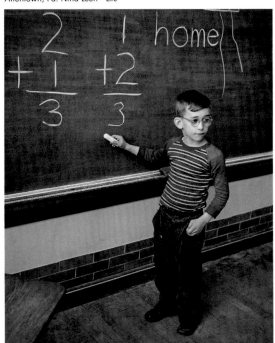

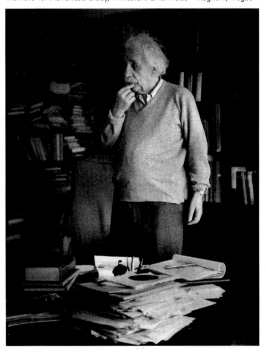

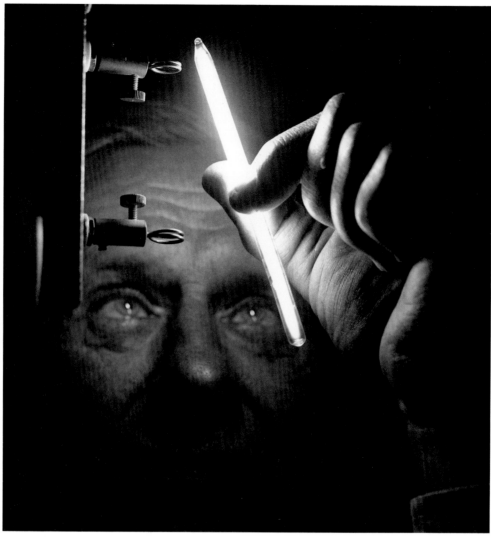

U.S.A. Andreas Feininger  *Life*

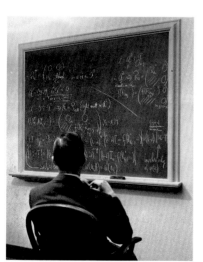

Inst. for Advanced Study, Princeton. Eisenstaedt

U.S.A. W. Eugene Smith  *Life*

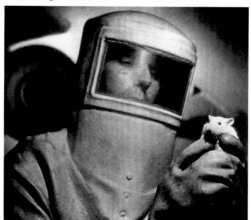

Radiation Laboratory, Univ. of Cal., Nat Farbman  *Life*

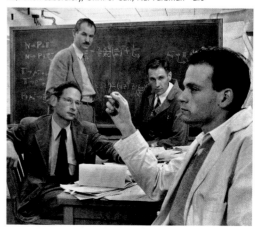

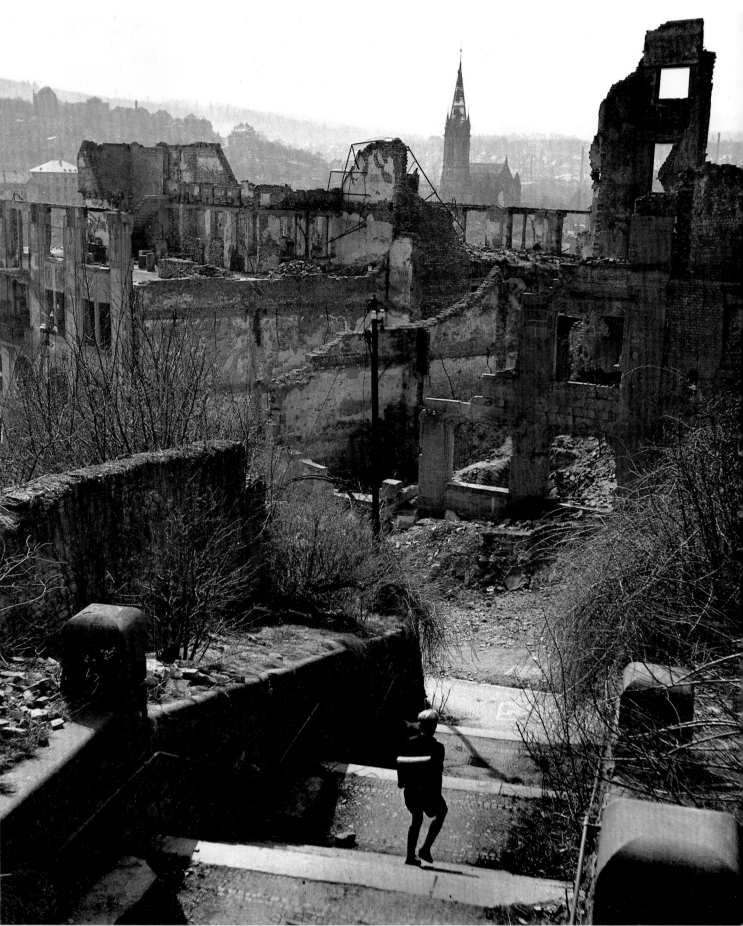

Germany. Otto Hagel

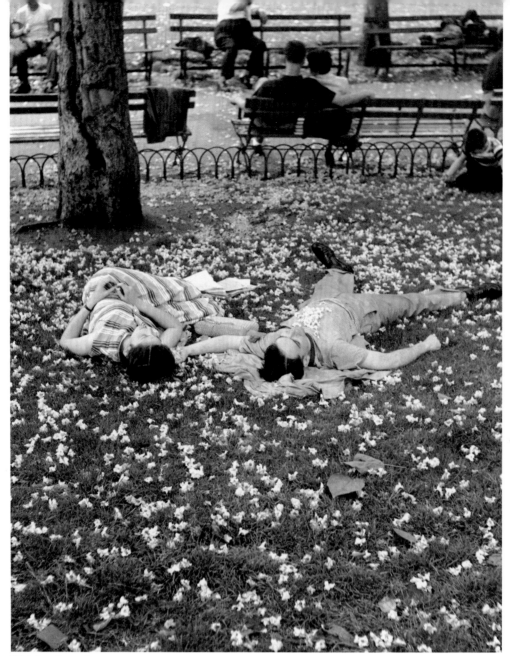

U.S.A. Ernst Haas  *Magnum*

*Every man beareth the whole stamp of the human condition.*  Montaigne

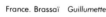

France. Brassaï  *Guillumette*

U.S.A. Alfred Eisenstaedt  *Life*

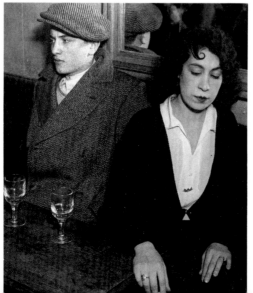

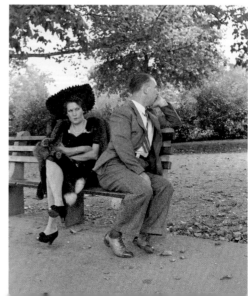

128

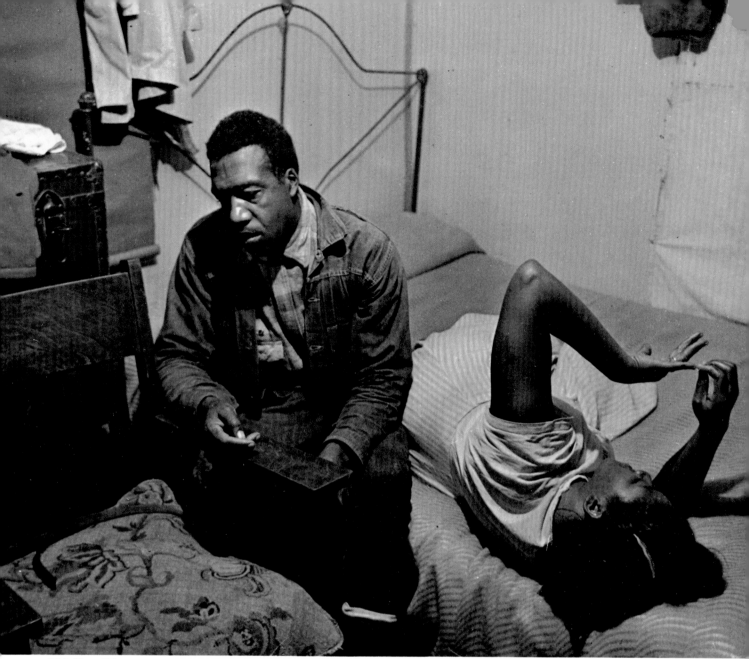

U.S.A. Wayne Miller

U.S.A. Dorothea Lange  *Fortune*

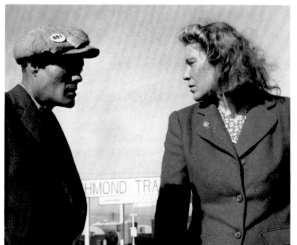

U.S.A. Harry Callahan

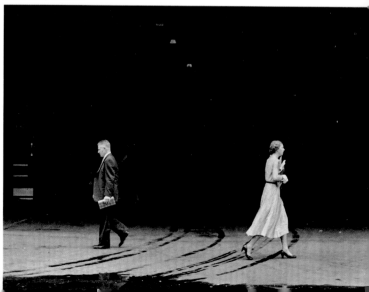

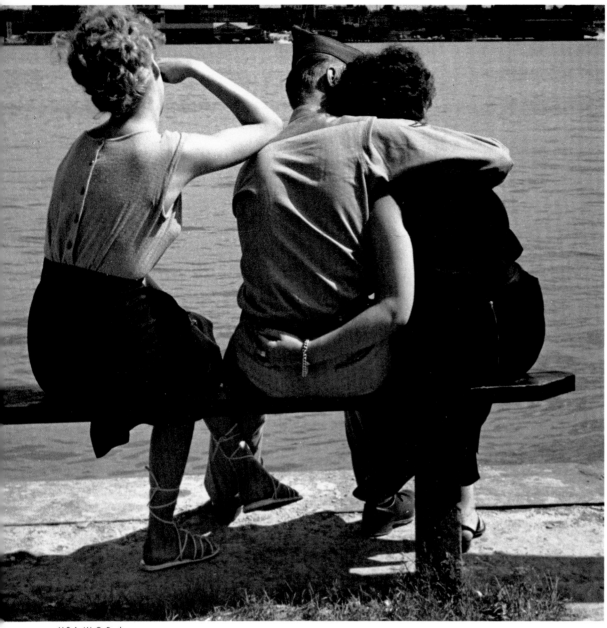

U.S.A. W. C. Rauhauser

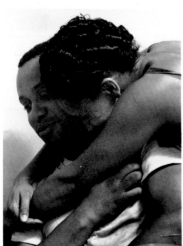

U.S.A. Roy De Carava

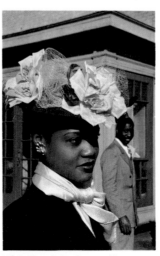

U.S.A. Henri Cartier-Bresson ·*Magnum*

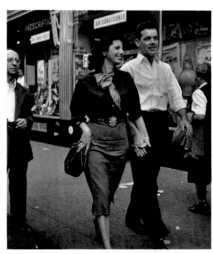

U.S.A. Homer Page

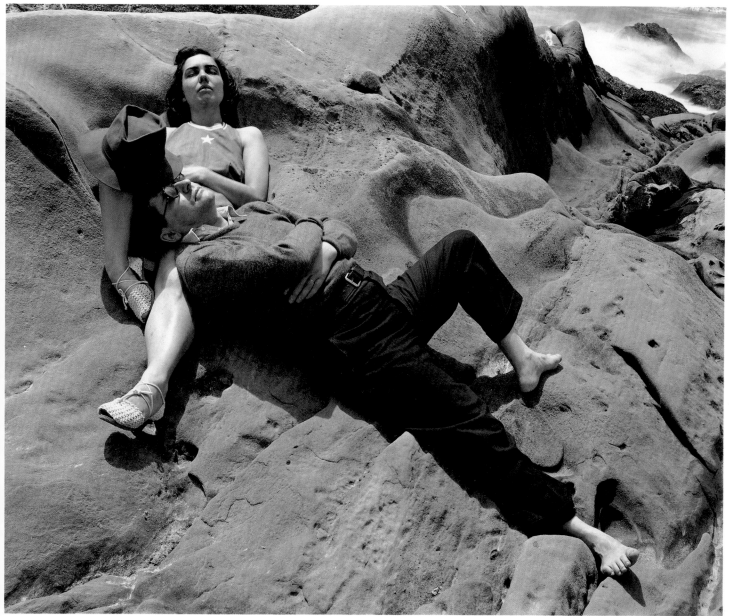

U.S.A. Edward Weston

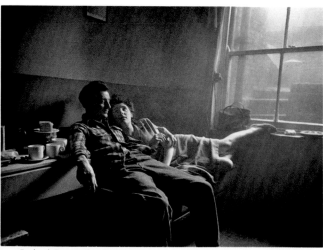

England. Bert Hardy  *Picture Post*

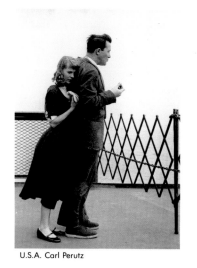

U.S.A. Carl Perutz

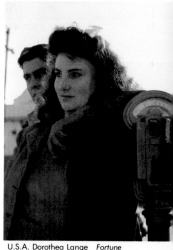

U.S.A. Dorothea Lange  *Fortune*

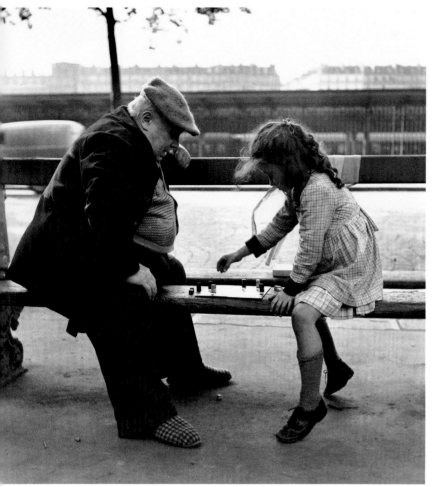

France. Fred Plaut

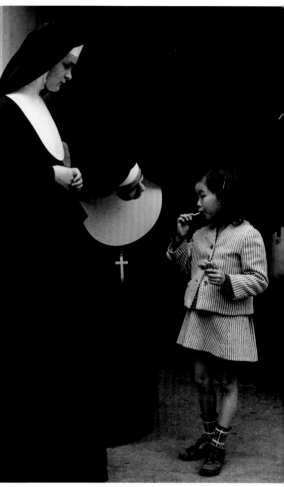

San Francisco. Ruth Marion Baruch

Sweden. Pal-Nils Nilsson

England. Cornell Capa  *Life*

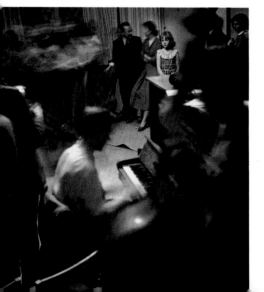

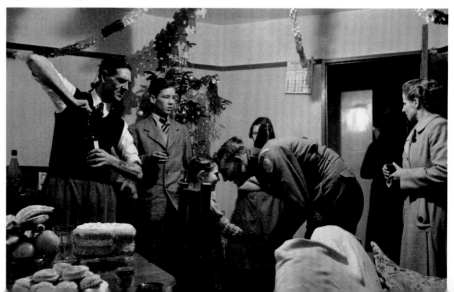

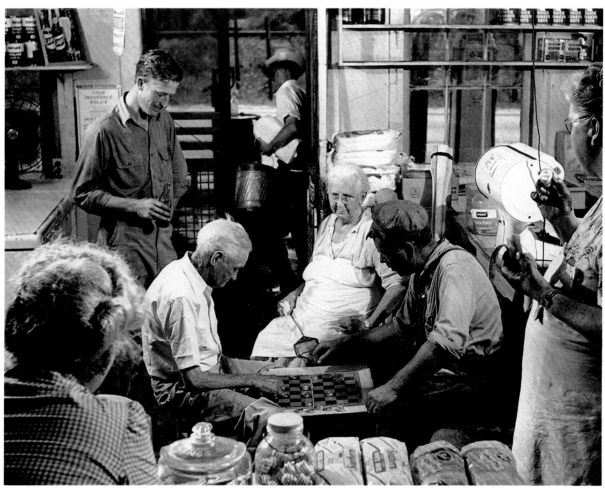

North Carolina, U.S.A. Ike Vern

U.S.A. Guy Gillette  *Brackman Associates*

Korea. Joseph Breitenbach  *United Nations*

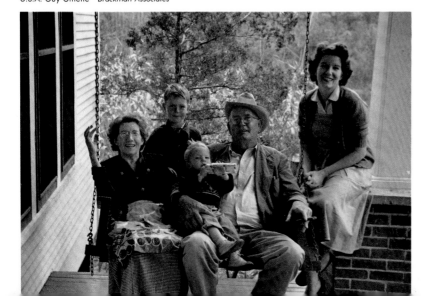

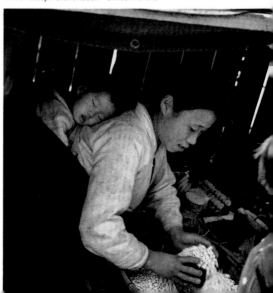

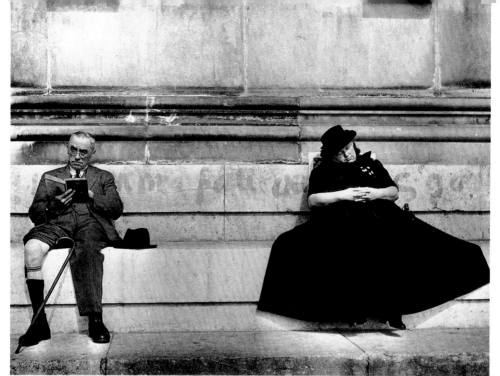

Germany. Herbert List   *Time Inc.*

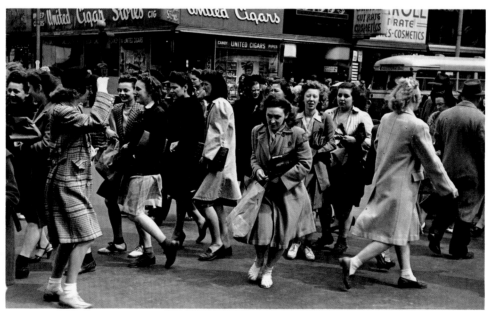

U.S.A. Peter Stackpole   *Life*

U.S.A. Garry Winogrand   *Brackman Assoc.*

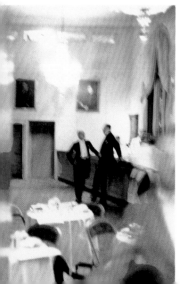

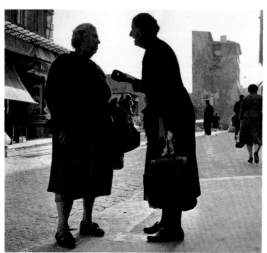

France. Peter Moeschlin

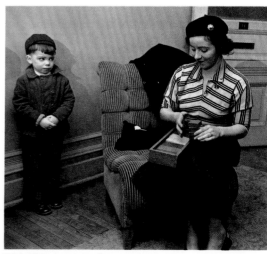

U.S.A. Victor Jorgensen   *Scope*

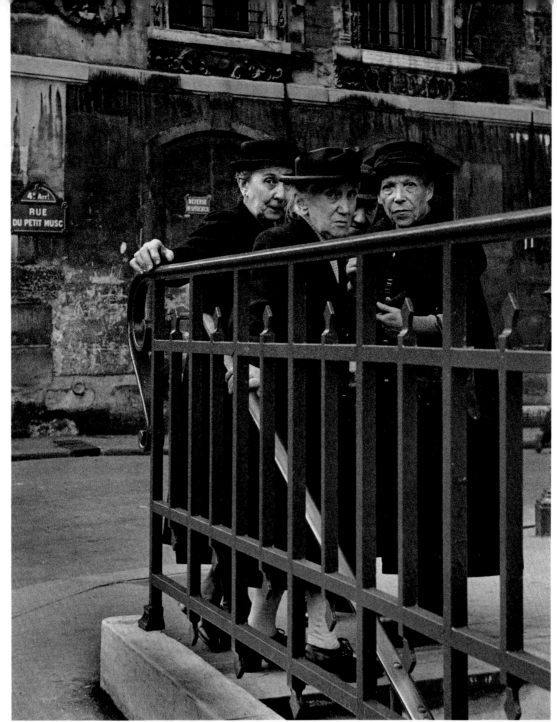

France. Jean Marquis  *Magnum*

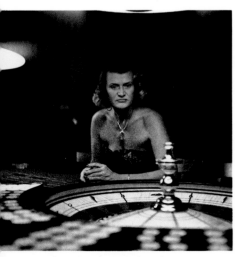

Puerto Rico. Gordon Parks  *Life*

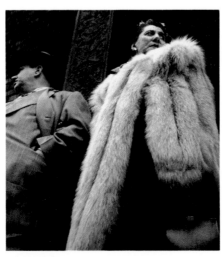
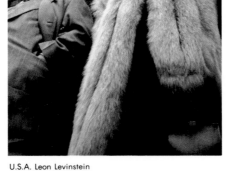

U.S.A. Leon Levinstein

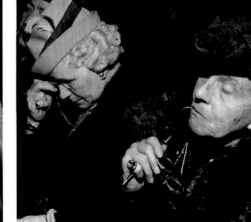

U.S.A. Lisette Model

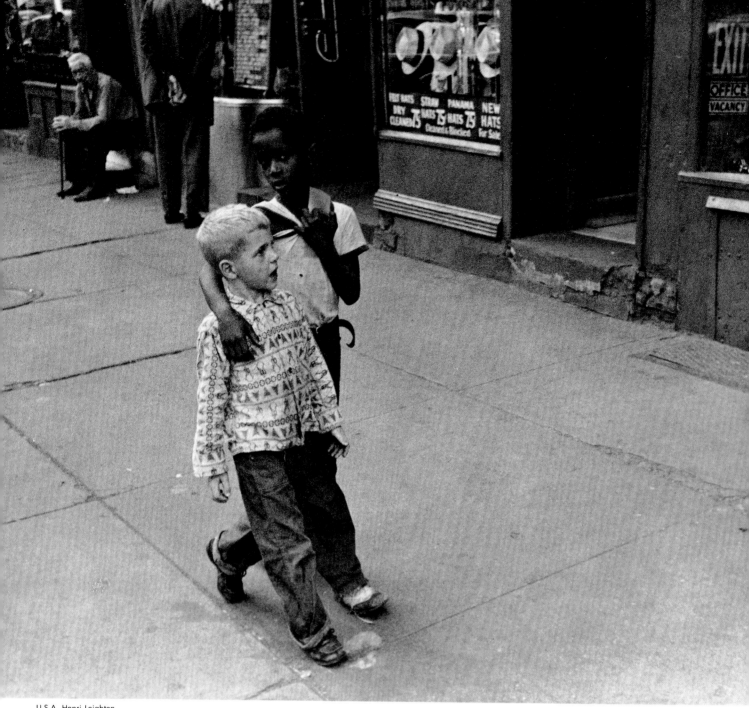

U.S.A. Henri Leighton

Germany. David Seymour  *Magnum, UNESCO*

France. Eleanor Fast

U.S.A. Allan Turoff

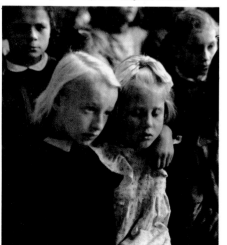

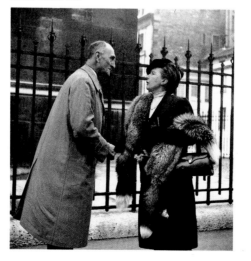

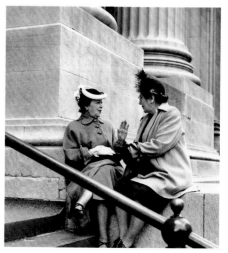

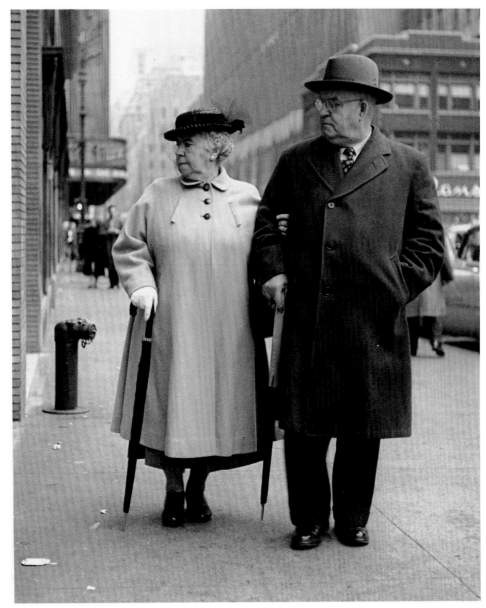

U.S.A. Mildred Grossman

France. Nat Farbman  *Life*

Germany. Ted Castle  *Magnum, AFSC*

Saudi Arabia. David Duncan  *Life*

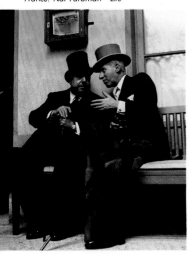

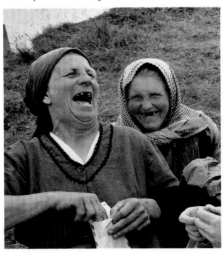

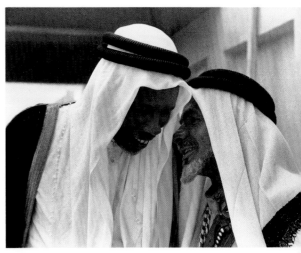

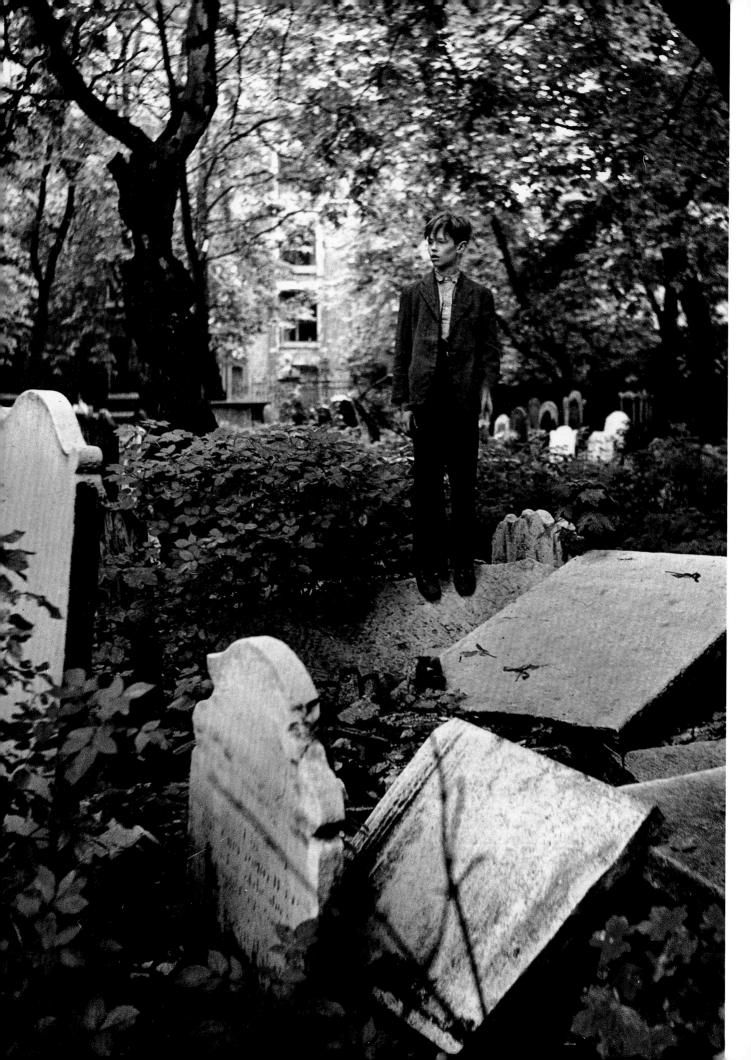

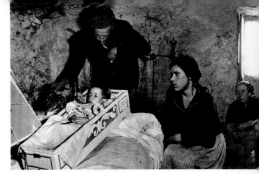
Spain. Leonti Planskoy

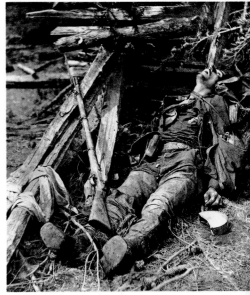
U.S.A. Mathew Brady, *circa 1861*

*As the generation of leaves,*

*so is that of men.*

Homer

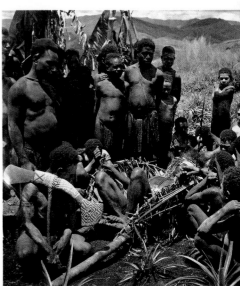
New Guinea. Arnold Maahs   *Black Star*

England. Keystone Press

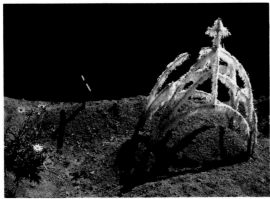
Mexico. Manuel Alvarez Bravo

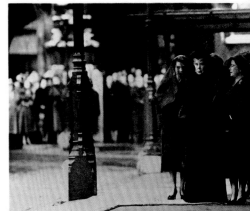

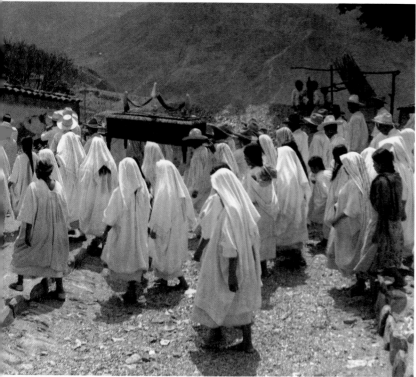

Mexico. Lola Alvarez Bravo

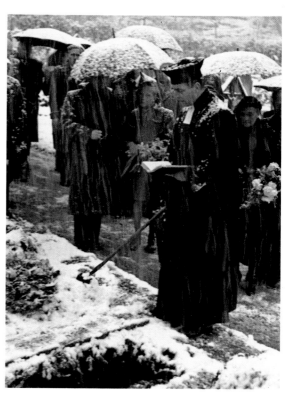

Germany. Willie Huttig

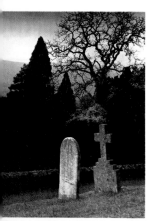

England. Bill Brandt

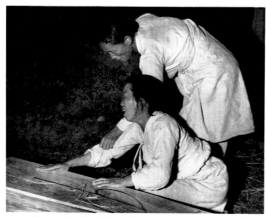

Korea. Margaret Bourke-White  *Life*

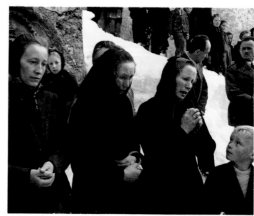

Austria. Robert Halmi

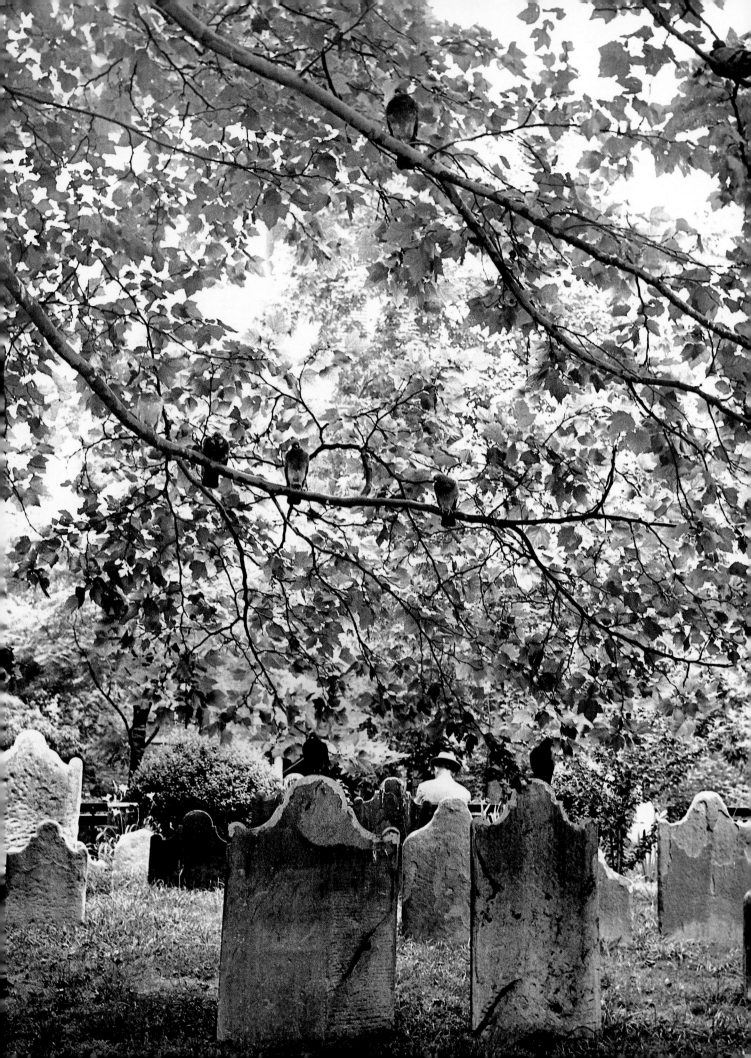

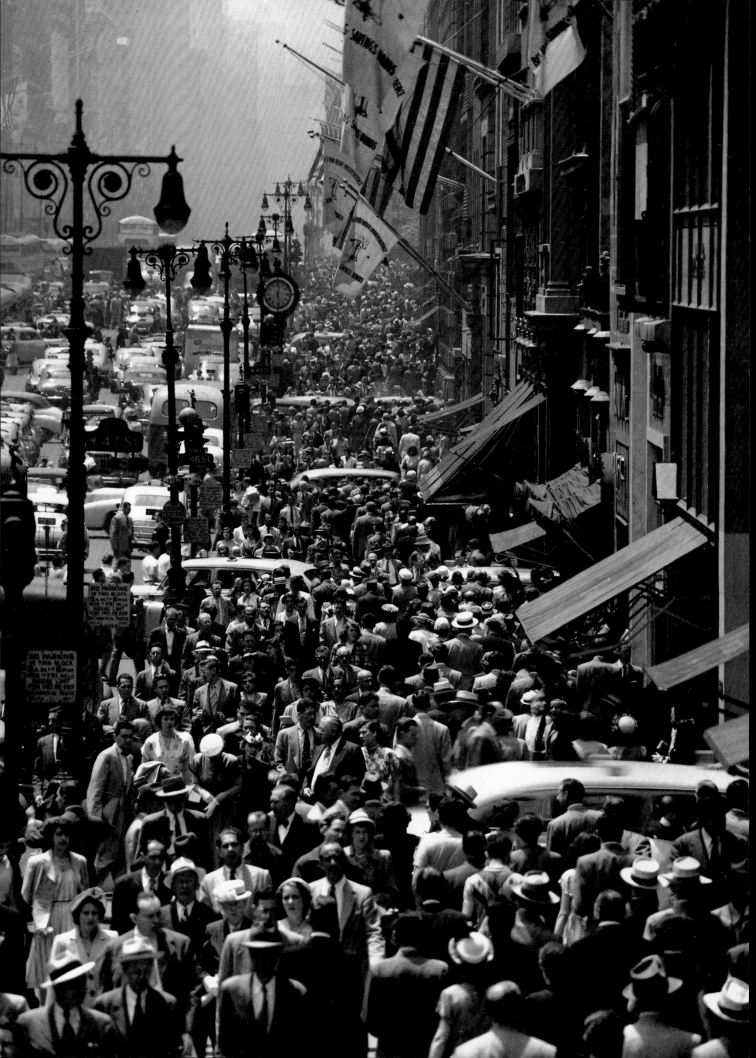

Sweden. Karl W. Gullers

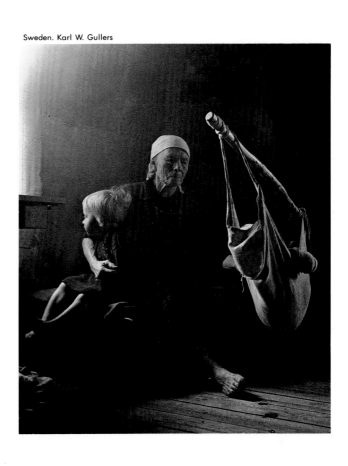

*Flow, flow, flow, the current of life is ever onward . . .*    Kobodaishi

Spain. Robert Frank

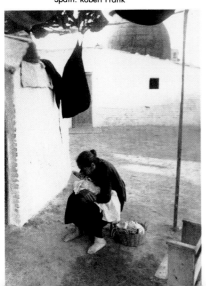

U.S.A. Rondal Partridge

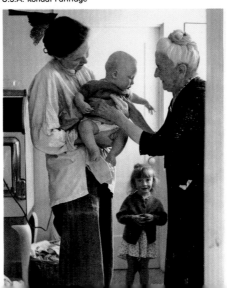

Germany. Mildred Grossman

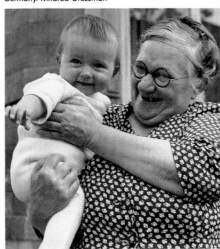

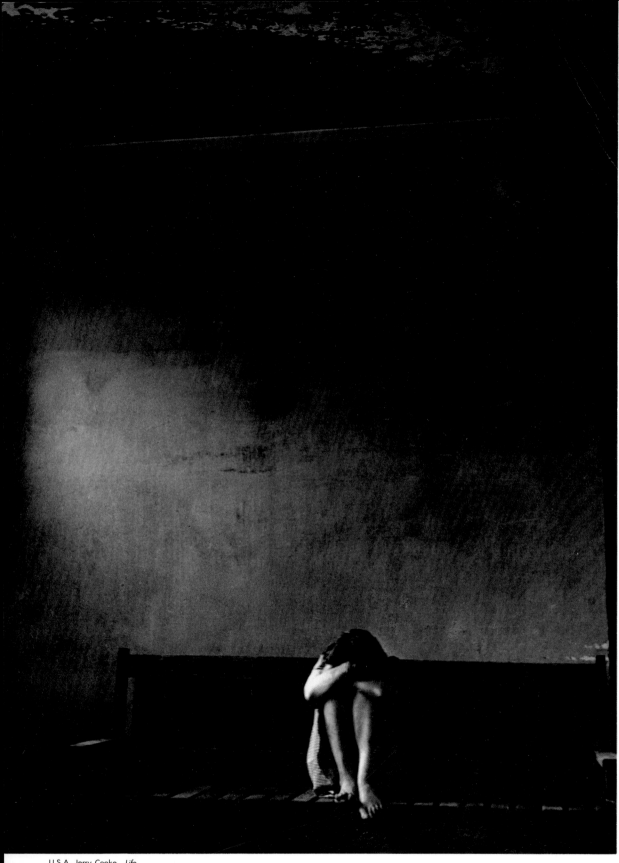

U.S.A. Jerry Cooke  *Life*

*...I am alone with the beating of my heart...*   Lui Chi

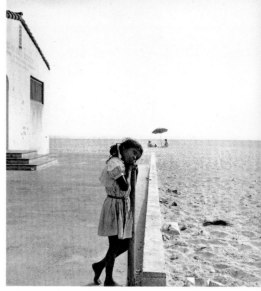

U.S.A. Louis Clyde Stoumen

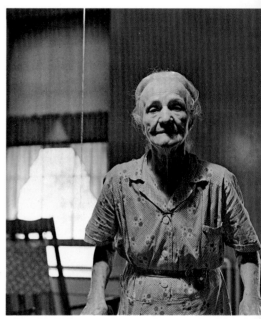

U.S.A. Daniel J. Ransohoff

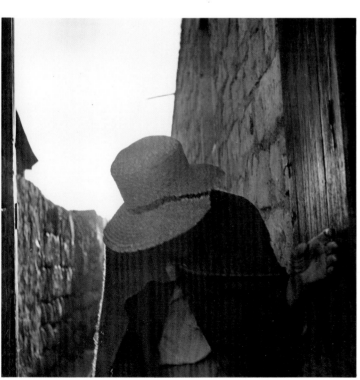

Peru. Robert Frank

U.S.A. Alfred Statler

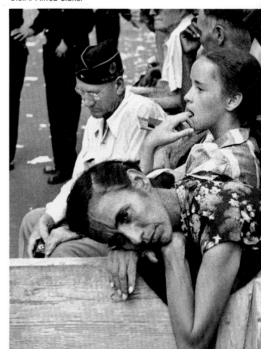

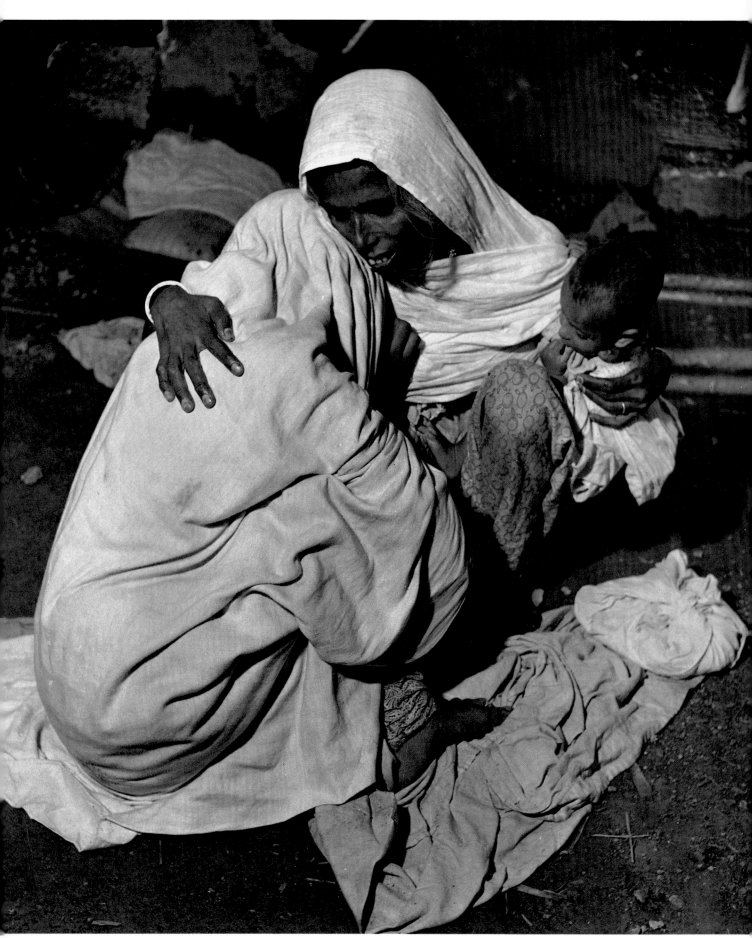

India. Margaret Bourke-White  *Life*

*For Mercy has a human heart,*

*Pity a human face . . . .*

William Blake

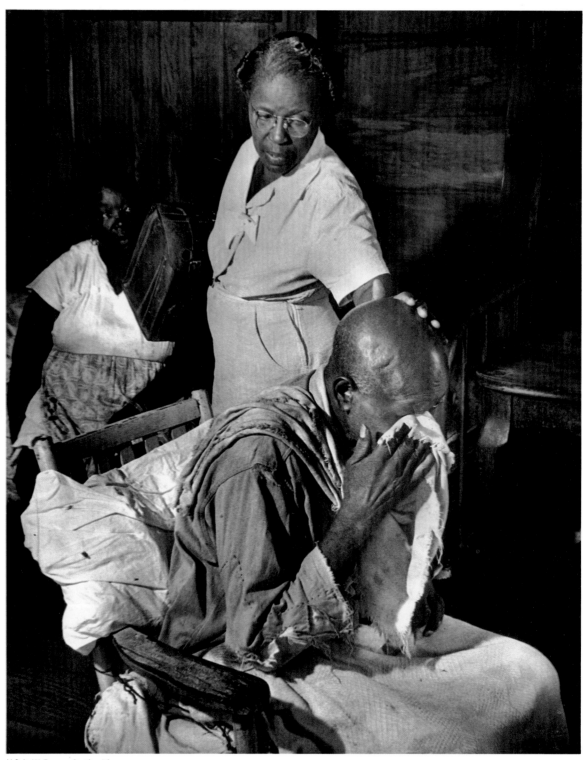

U.S.A. W. Eugene Smith  *Life*

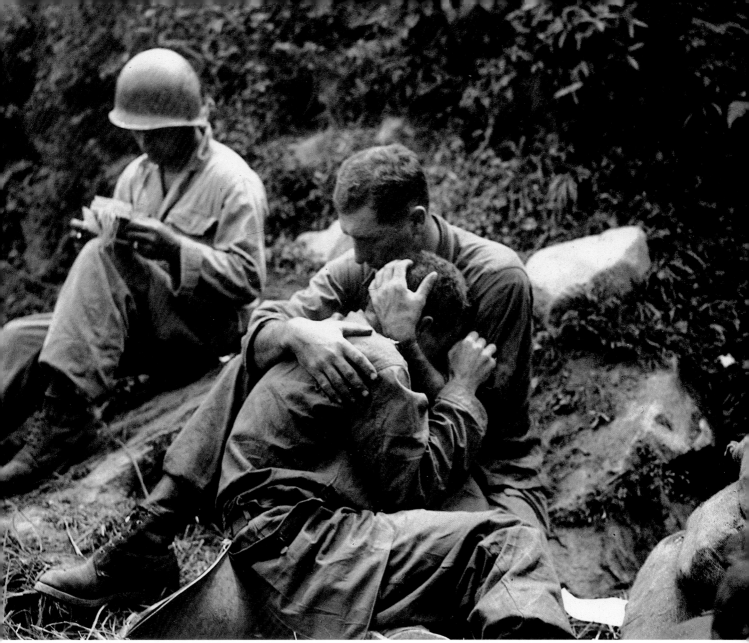

Korea. U.S. Signal Corps, Al Chang

Jamaica. George Silk  *Life*

Greece. D. Harrissiades  *Life*

India. Gitel Steed

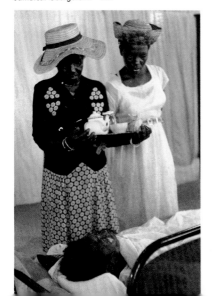

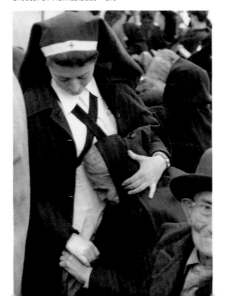

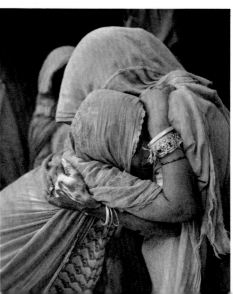

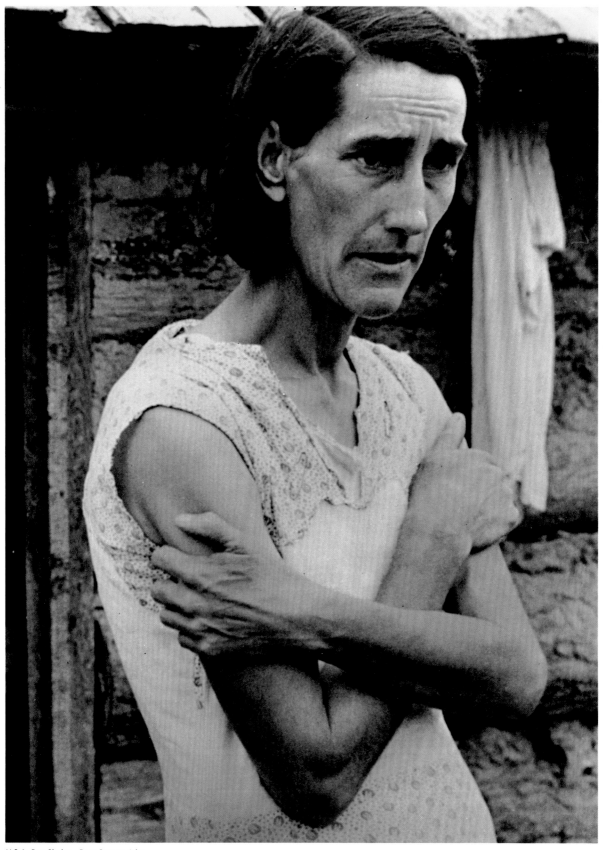

U.S.A. Ben Shahn   *Farm Security Adm.*

*What region of the earth is not full of our calamities?*   Virgil

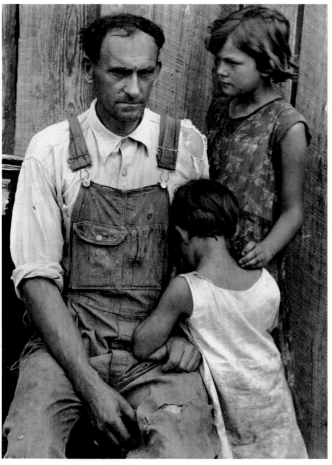

U.S.A. Doris Ulmann

U.S.A. Dorothea Lange

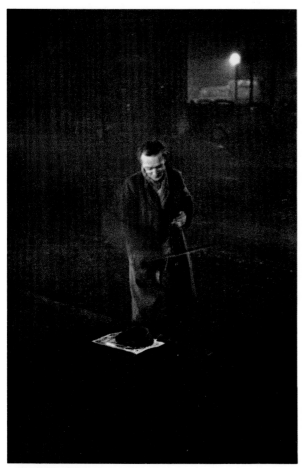

England. Robert Frank

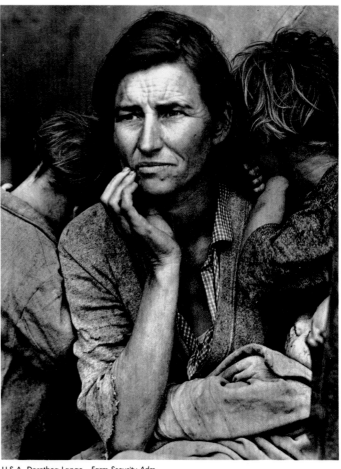

U.S.A. Dorothea Lange   *Farm Security Adm.*

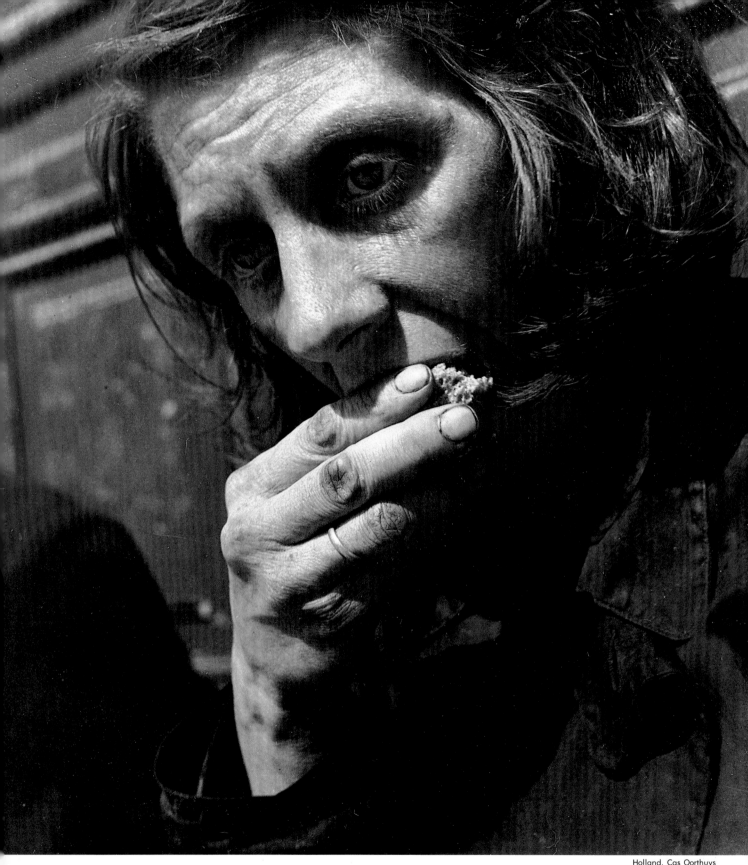

Holland. Cas Oorthuys

*. . . Nothing is real to us but hunger.*  Kakuzo Okakura

India. William Vandivert  *Life*
China. George Silk  *Life*
India. Werner Bischof  *Magnum*
India. Constantin Joffé  *Vogue*
Arctic. Richard Harrington  *Three Lions*

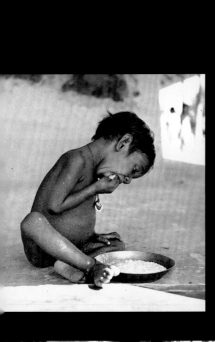
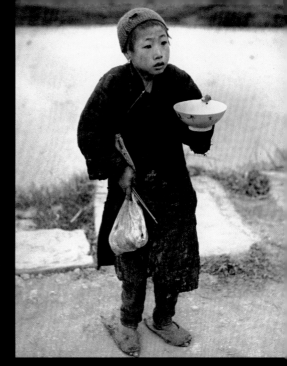
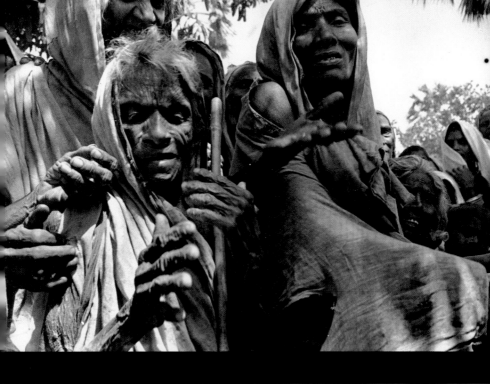
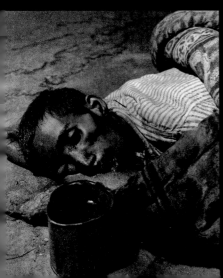
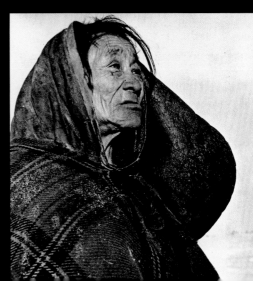

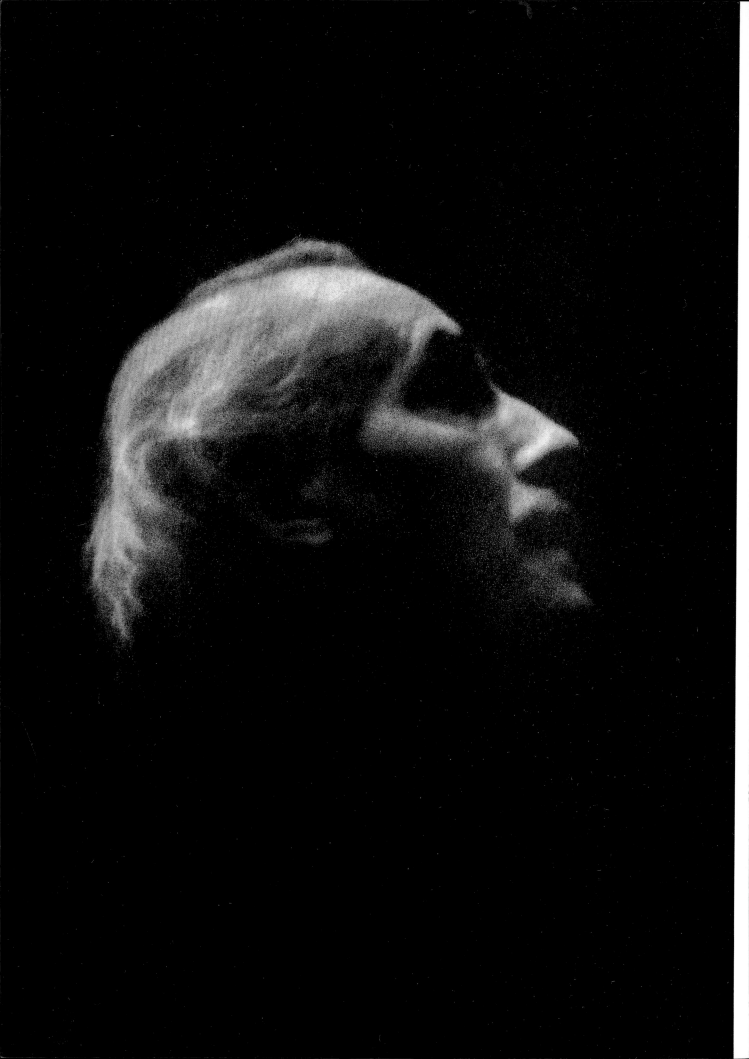

Wales. Robert Frank

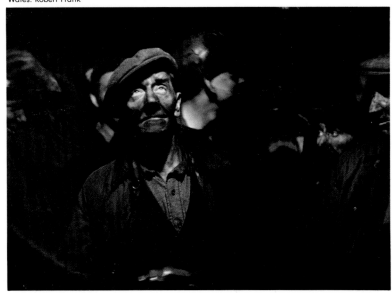

*Behold, this dreamer cometh*     Genesis 37:19

U.S.A. Nell Dorr

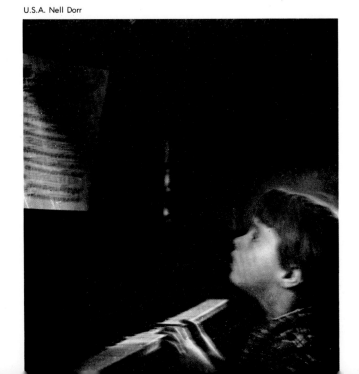

U.S.A. Homer Page

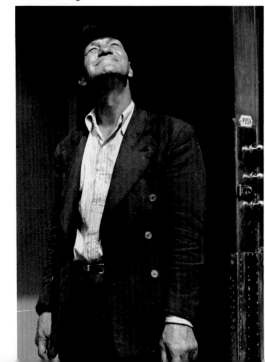

..... *To know that what is impenetrable to us really exists, manifesting*

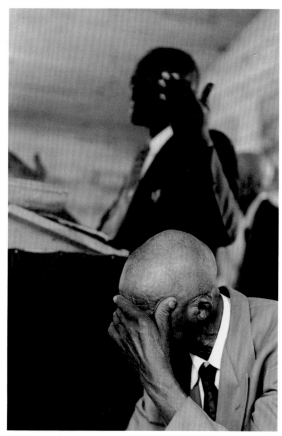

U.S.A. Elliott Erwitt   *Magnum, Holiday*

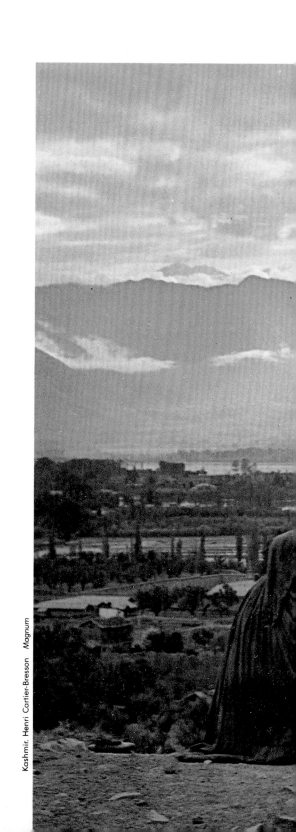

Kashmir. Henri Cartier-Bresson   *Magnum*

*itself as the highest wisdom and the most radiant beauty . . .*     Albert Einstein

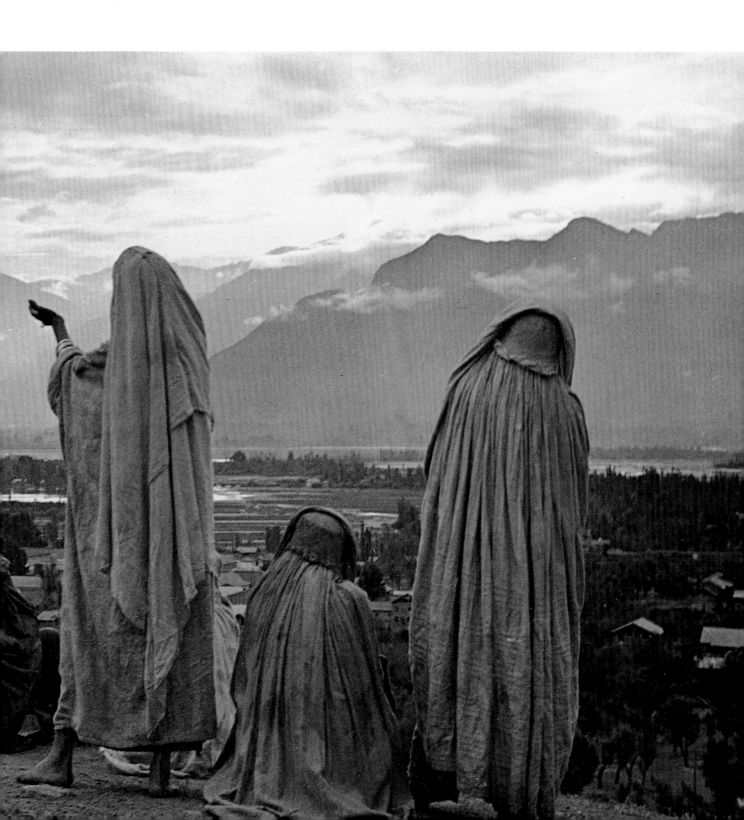

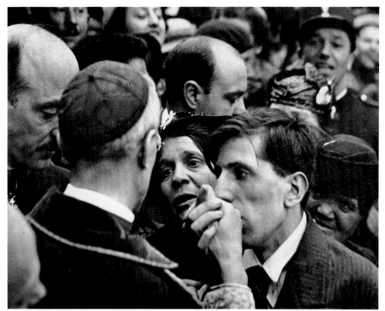

France. Henri Cartier-Bresson  *Magnum*

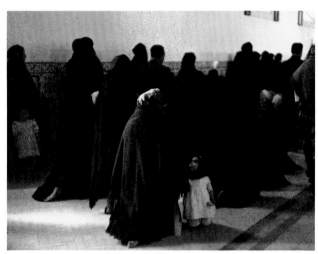

Portugal. Sabine Weiss  *Rapho Guillumette*

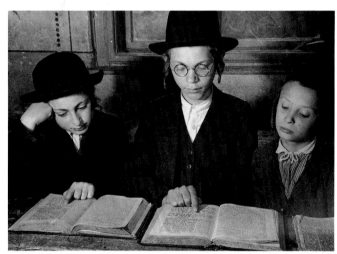

Czechoslovakia. Margaret Bourke-White  *Life*

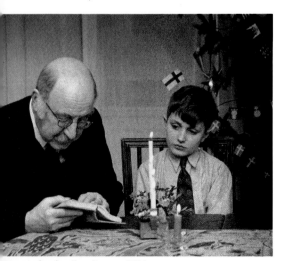

Sweden. Hans Hammarskjöld

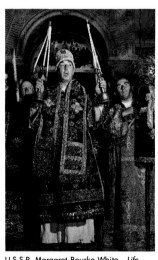

U.S.S.R. Margaret Bourke-White  *Life*

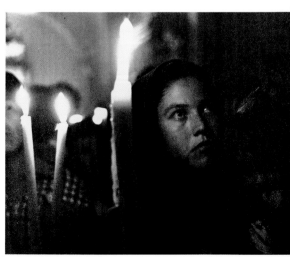

Mexico. May Mirin  *Jubilee*

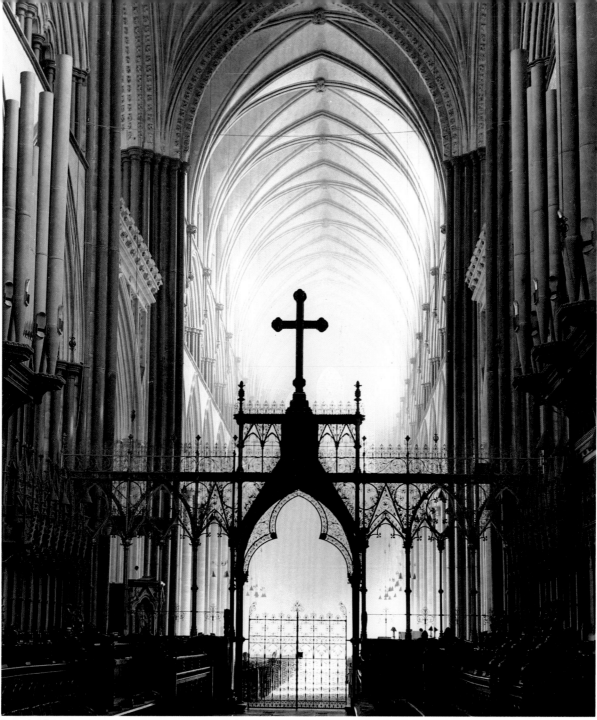

England. Bill Brandt

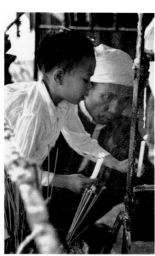

Burma. Bert Hardy   Pix, Picture Post

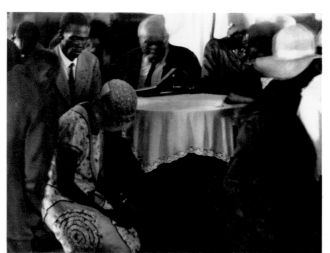

U.S.A. Doris Ulmann

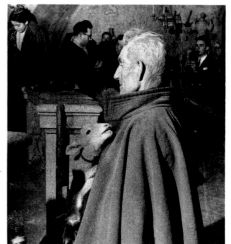

France. Brassaï   Rapho Guillumette

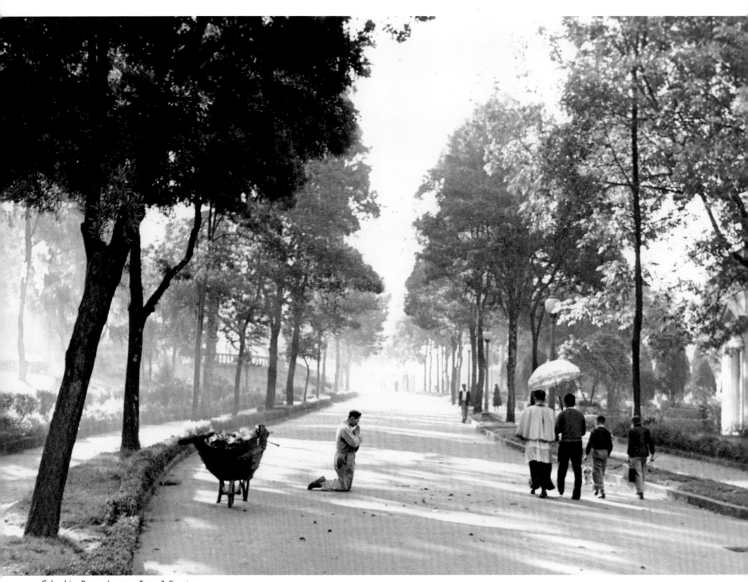

Colombia. Ronny Jaques  *Town & Country*

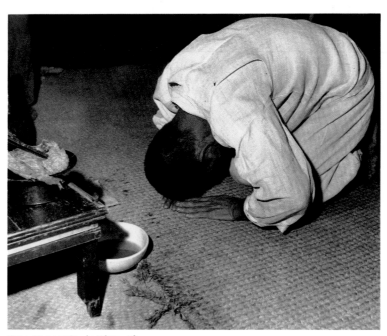

Korea. Margaret Bourke-White   *Life*

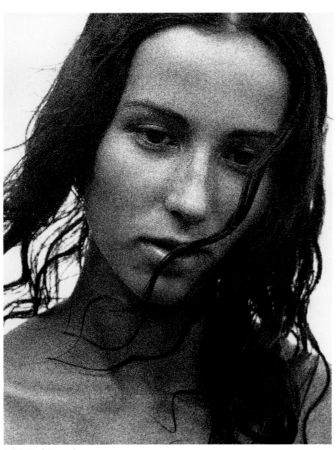

U.S.A. Paul Himmel

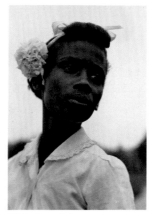

U.S.A. Consuelo Kanaga

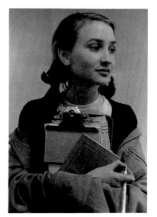

U.S.A. A. Marshak  *U.S. State Dept.*

*. . . . I still believe that people are*

U.S.A. Esther Bubley  *Ladies' Home Journal*

U.S.A. Margery Lewis  *Seventeen*

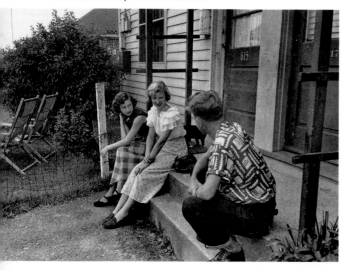

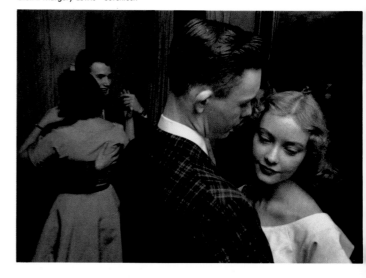

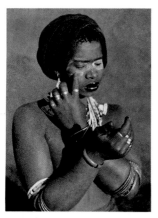
South Africa. Constance Stuart *Black Star*

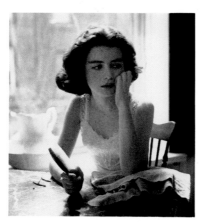
U.S.A. Tana Hoban *Rapho Guillumette*

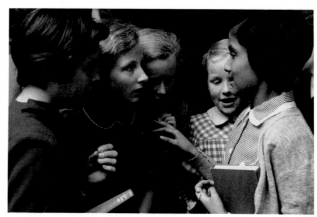
England. Esther Bubley *Life*

*really good at heart.*

Anne Frank, "Diary" (14 years old)

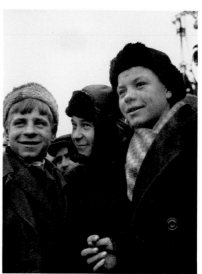
Moscow. Thomas McAvoy *Life*

Yugoslavia. Fenno Jacobs *Black Star*

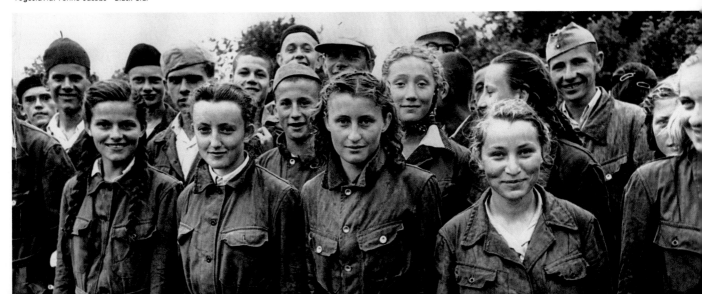

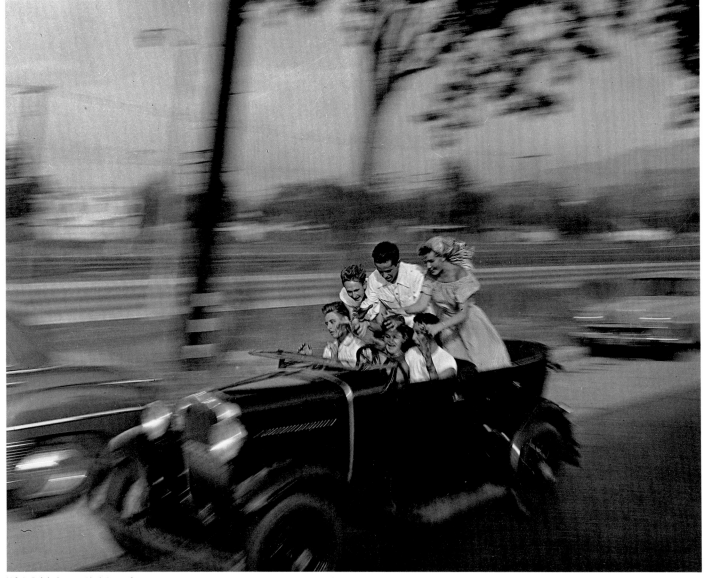

U.S.A. Ralph Crane  *Black Star, Life*

*You are the young wonder-tree plant, grown out of ruins.*  Baronga—African Folk Tale

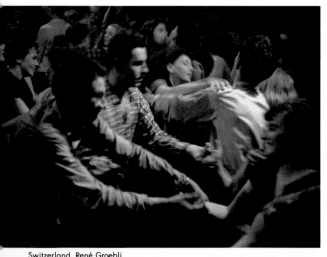

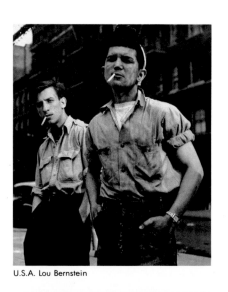

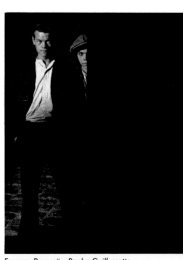

Switzerland. René Groebli

U.S.A. Lou Bernstein

France. Brassaï  *Rapho Guillumette*

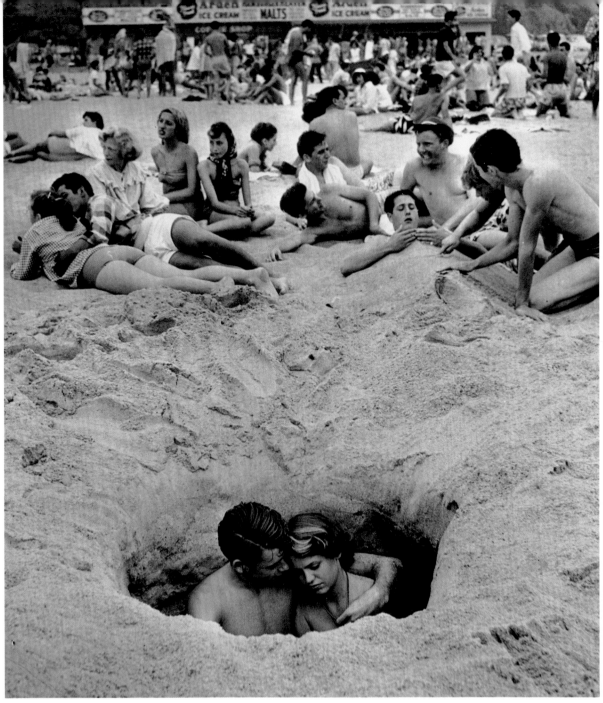

U.S.A. Ralph Crane  *Black Star, Life*

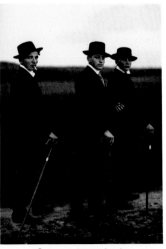

Germany. August Sander

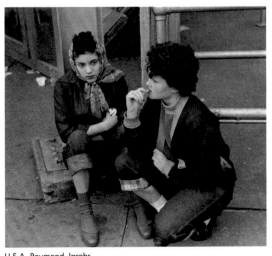

U.S.A. Raymond Jacobs

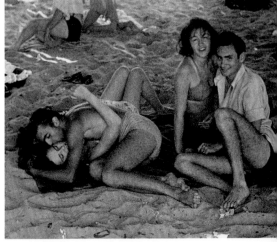

U.S.A. Fritz Neugass

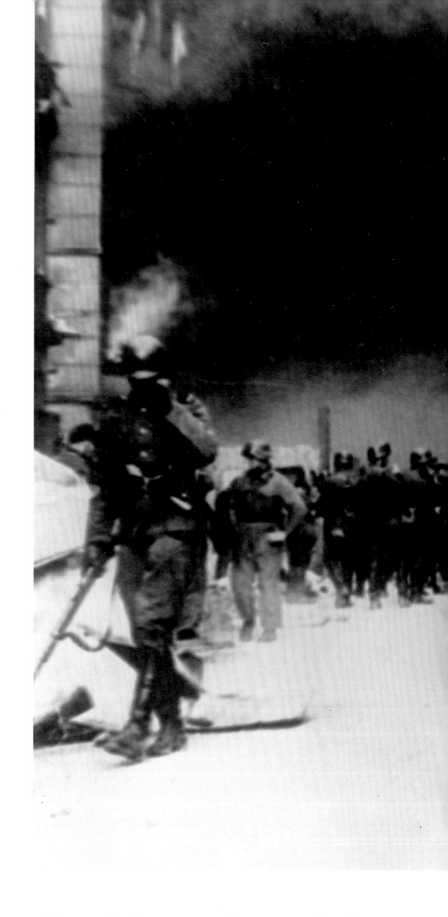

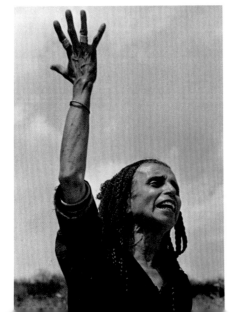

Israel. Anna Riwkin-Brick

*. . . Humanity is outraged in me and with me.*

*We must not dissimulate nor try to forget this*

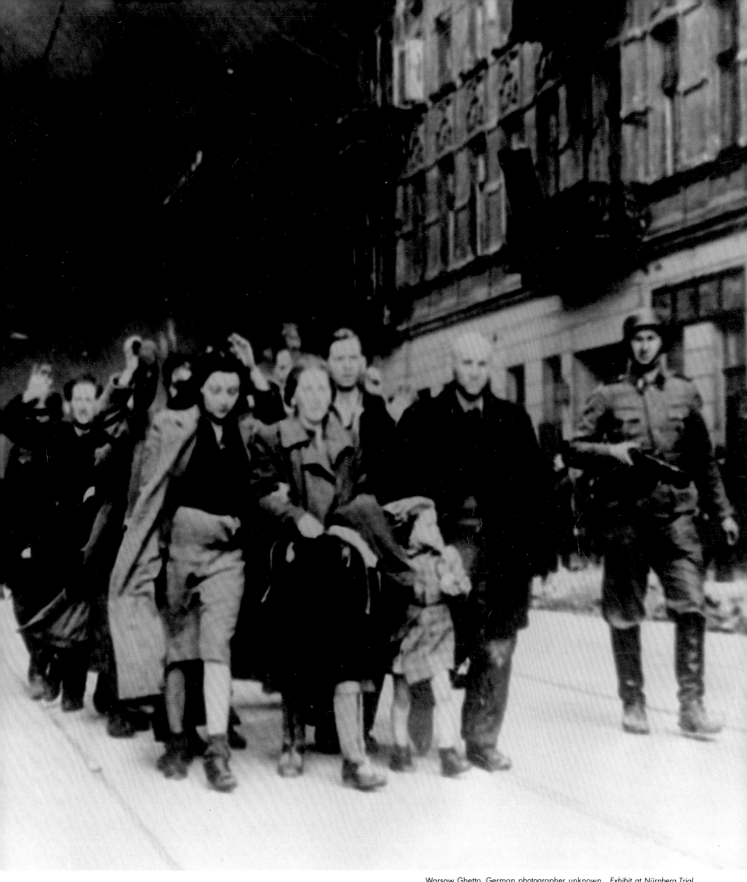

Warsaw Ghetto. German photographer unknown    *Exhibit at Nürnberg Trial*

*indignation which is one of the most passionate forms of love.*

George Sand

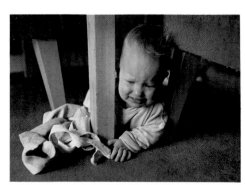

U.S.A. Wayne Miller  *Ladies' Home Journal*

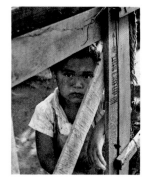

U.S.A. Marion Palfi

*. . . the mind is restless, turbulent, strong and unyielding . . .*

*as difficult to subdue as the wind.*     Bhagavad-Gita

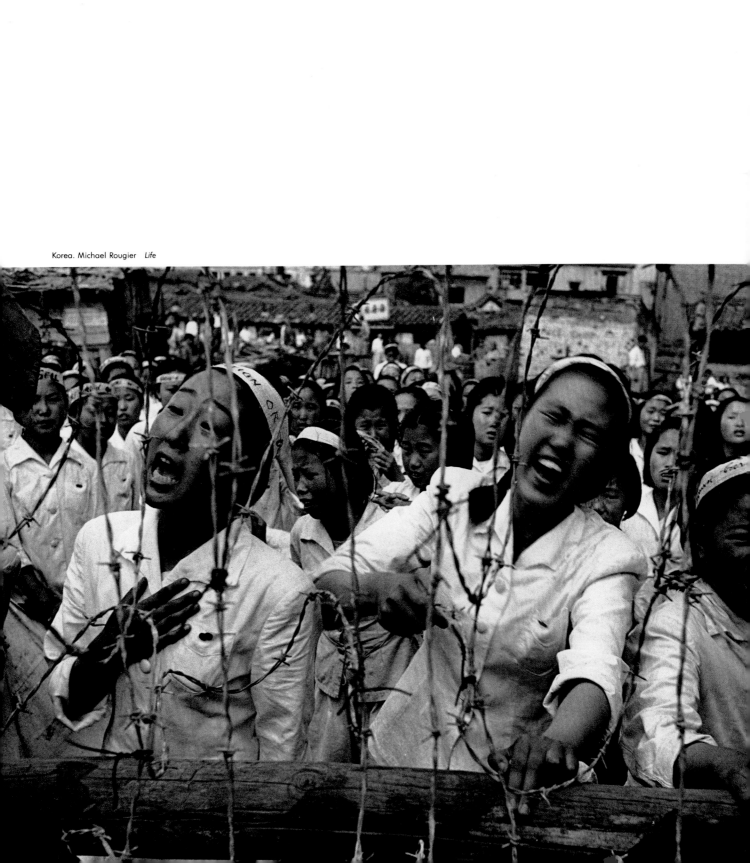

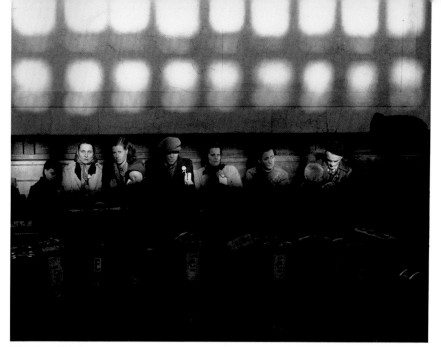

U.S.A. Carmel Vitullo

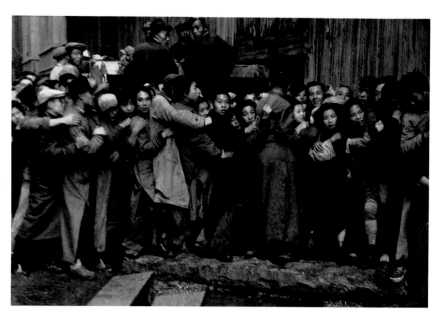

Shanghai, China. Henri Cartier-Bresson  *Magnum*

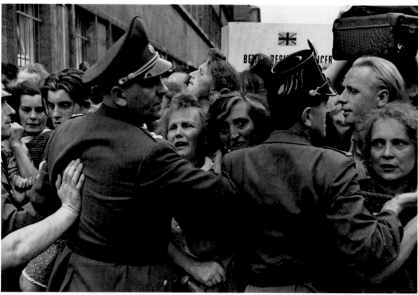

Germany. Ralph Crane  *Life*

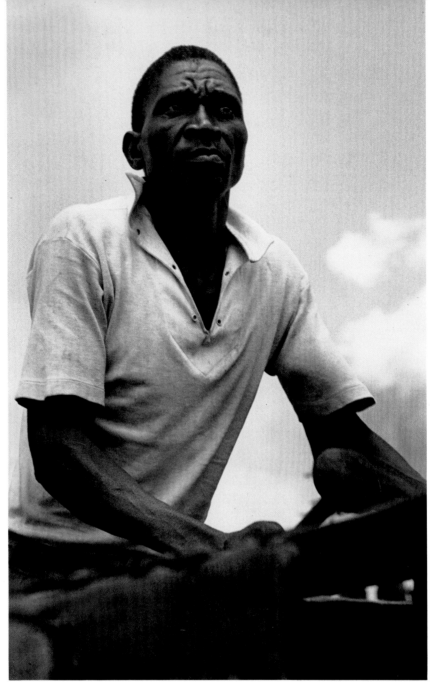

South Africa. Homer Page

*Who is on my side? Who?*     II. Kings 9:32

Indonesia. John Florea  *Life*

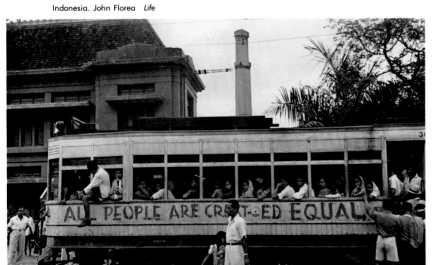

Germany. Photographer unknown  *AP*

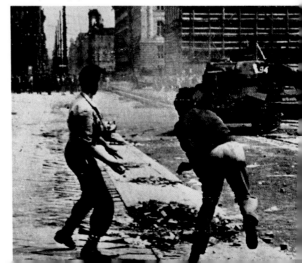

France. Nat Farbman *Life*

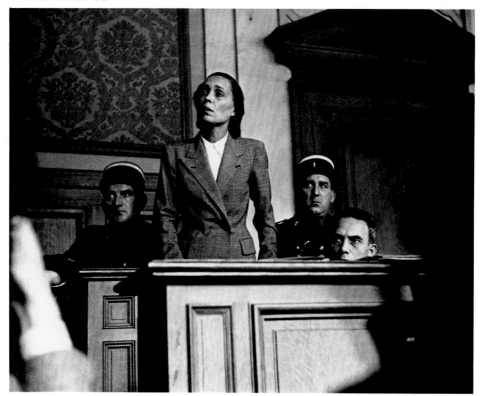

*Fill the seats of justice*

*With good men, not so absolute in goodness*

*As to forget what human frailty is.*

Sir Thomas Noon Talfourd

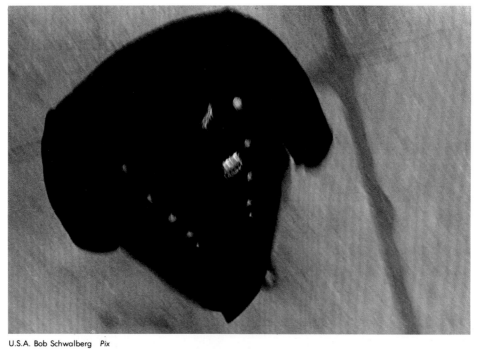

U.S.A. Bob Schwalberg *Pix*

U.S.A. Dan Weiner *Brackman Assoc., Fortune*

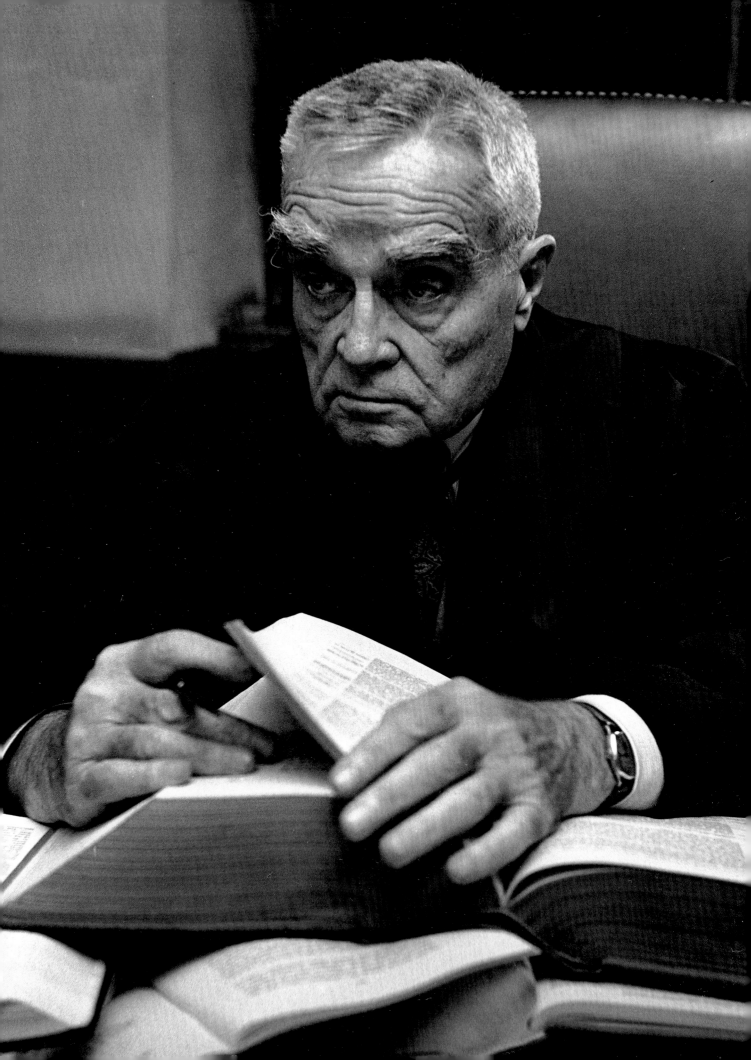

U.S.A. Sam Falk   *New York Times Magazine*

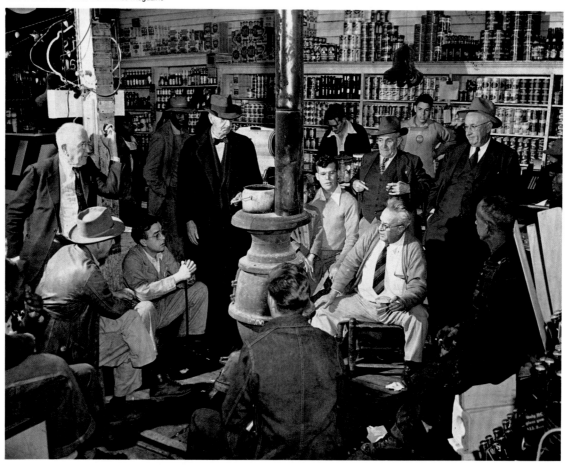

*I know no safe despository of the ultimate powers of society*

*but the people themselves . . .*     Thomas Jefferson

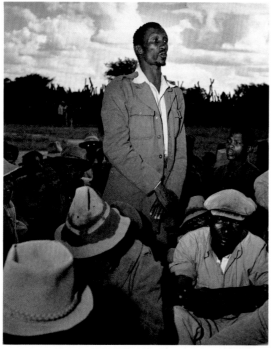

South Africa. Margaret Bourke-White   *Life*

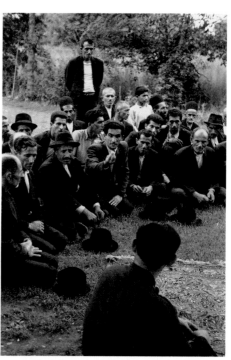

Iran. Henri Cartier-Bresson   *Magnum*

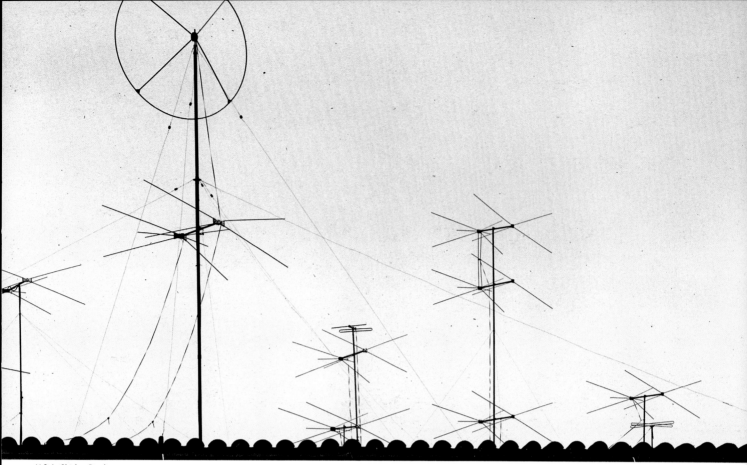

U.S.A. Shirley Burden

U.S.A. Edmund Bert Gerard  *Life*

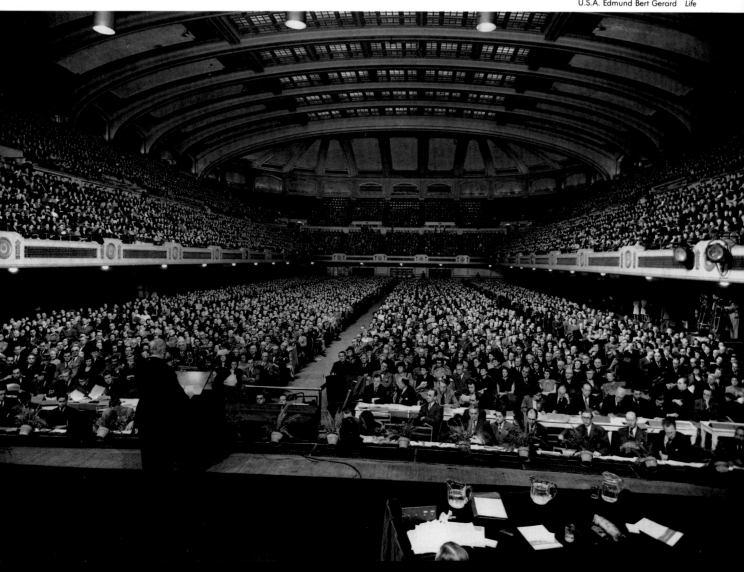

*Behold this and always love it! It is very sacred,*

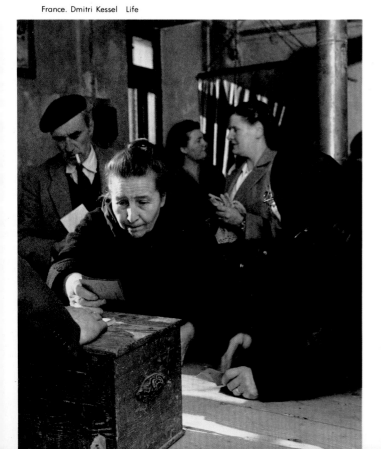

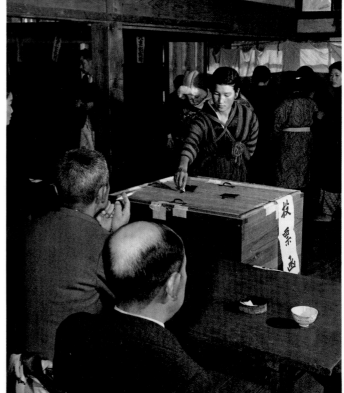

*and you must treat it as such . . .*

Sioux Indian

China. *Eastfoto*

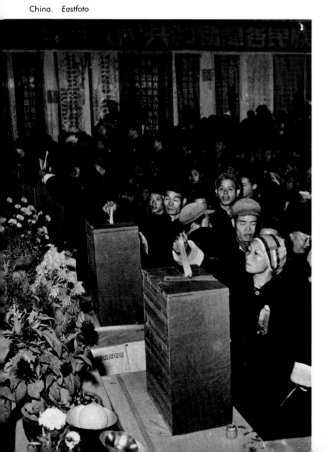

Turkey. Herman Kreider *Black Star*

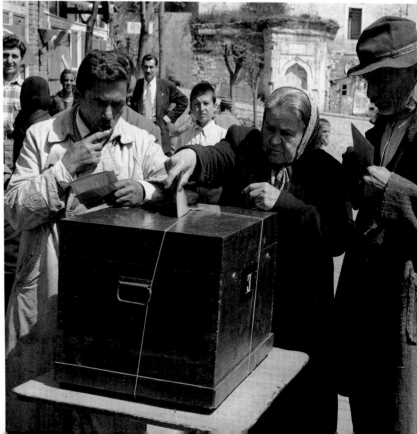

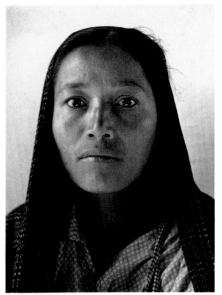

Mexico. Reva Brooks

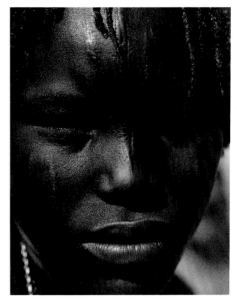

Africa. Peter W. Haberlin   *Du*

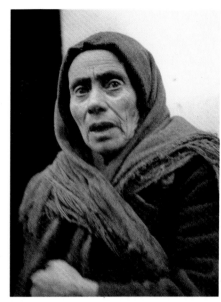

Poland. Roman Vishniac

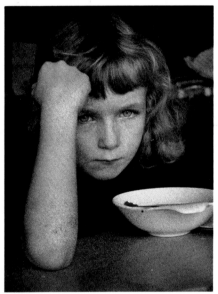

U.S.A. Joan Miller

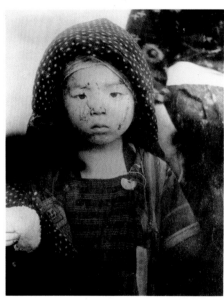

Nagasaki, Japan. Yosuke Yamahata   *G. T. Sun Co.*

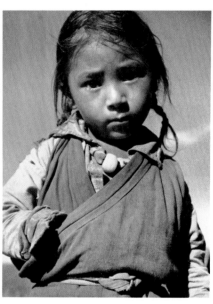

Indochina. Werner Bischof

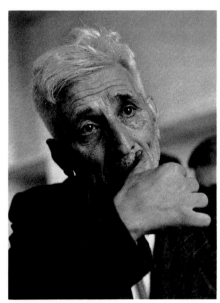

Italy. Ernst Haas   *Magnum*

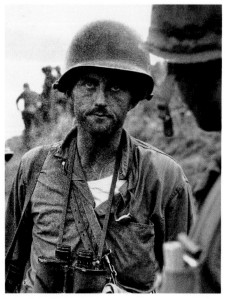

Korea. David Duncan   *Life*

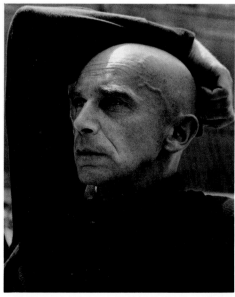

Austria. Yoichi Okamoto   *Popular Photography*

*. . . the best authorities are unanimous*

*in saying that a war with hydrogen bombs*

*is quite likely to put an end to the human race.*

*. . . there will be universal death—*

*sudden only for a fortunate minority,*

*but for the majority*

*a slow torture of disease and disintegration . . .*

Bertrand Russell

*Who is the slayer, who the victim? Speak.*

Sophocles

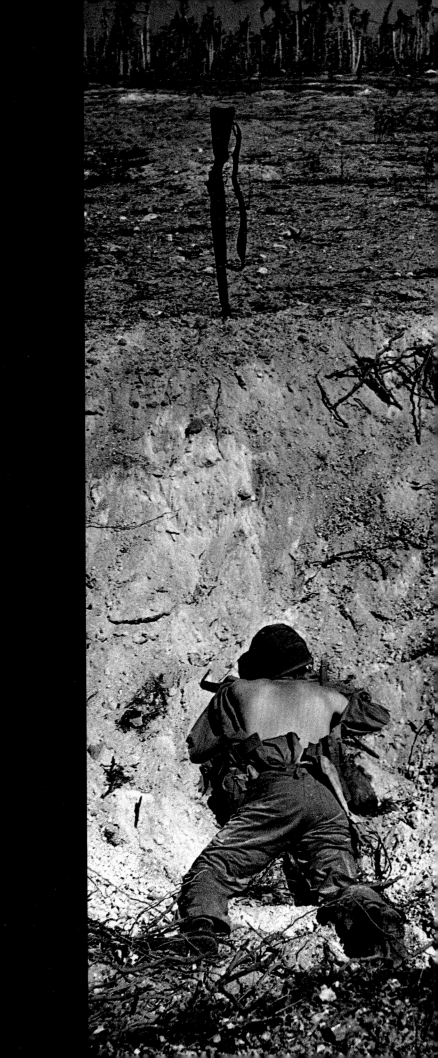

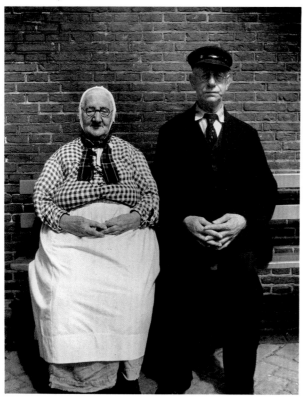

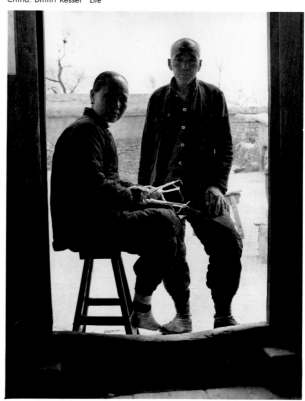

*We two form a multitude.*

*We two form a multitude.*

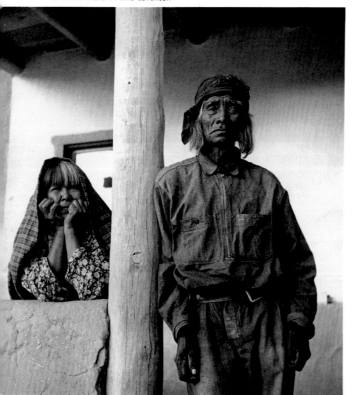

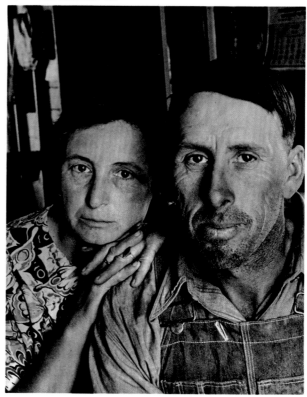

*We two form a multitude.*

*We two form a multitude.*

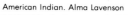

*Photograph on Page 181—Eniwetok. Raphel Platnick PHC. United States Coast Guard*

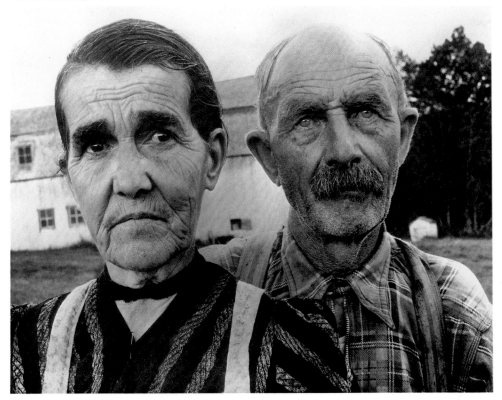

*We two form a multitude.*

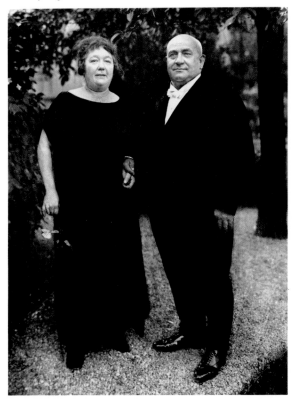

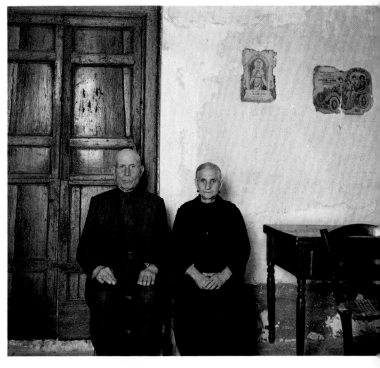

*We two form a multitude.*

*We two form a multitude.*    Ovid

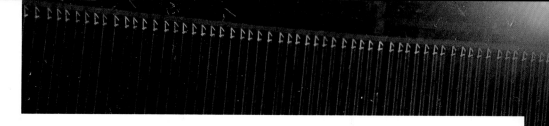

*We, the peoples of United Nations*
*Determined to save succeeding generations from the scourge of war,*
*which twice in our lifetime has brought untold sorrow to mankind, and*
*To reaffirm faith in fundamental human rights, in the dignity*
*and worth of the human person, in the equal rights of men and*
*women and of nations large and small . . .* Charter of the United Nations

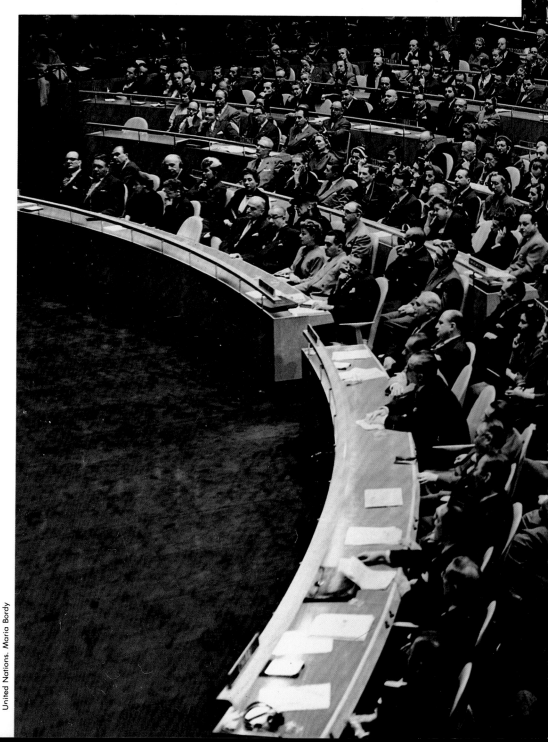

United Nations. Maria Bordy

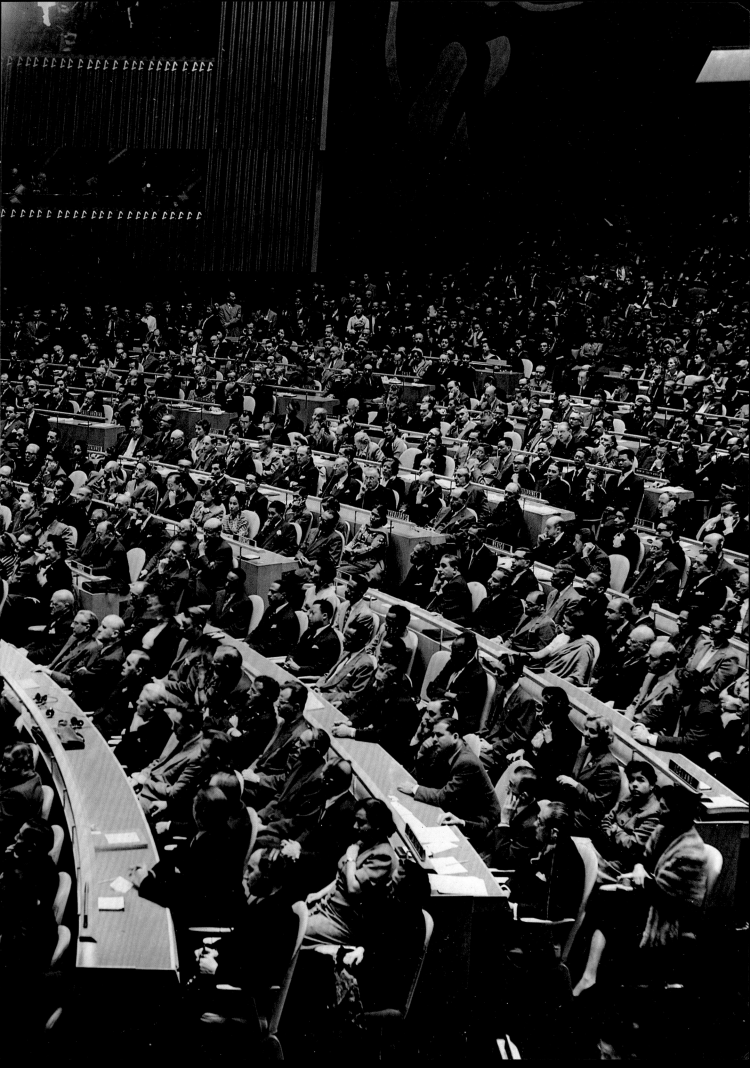

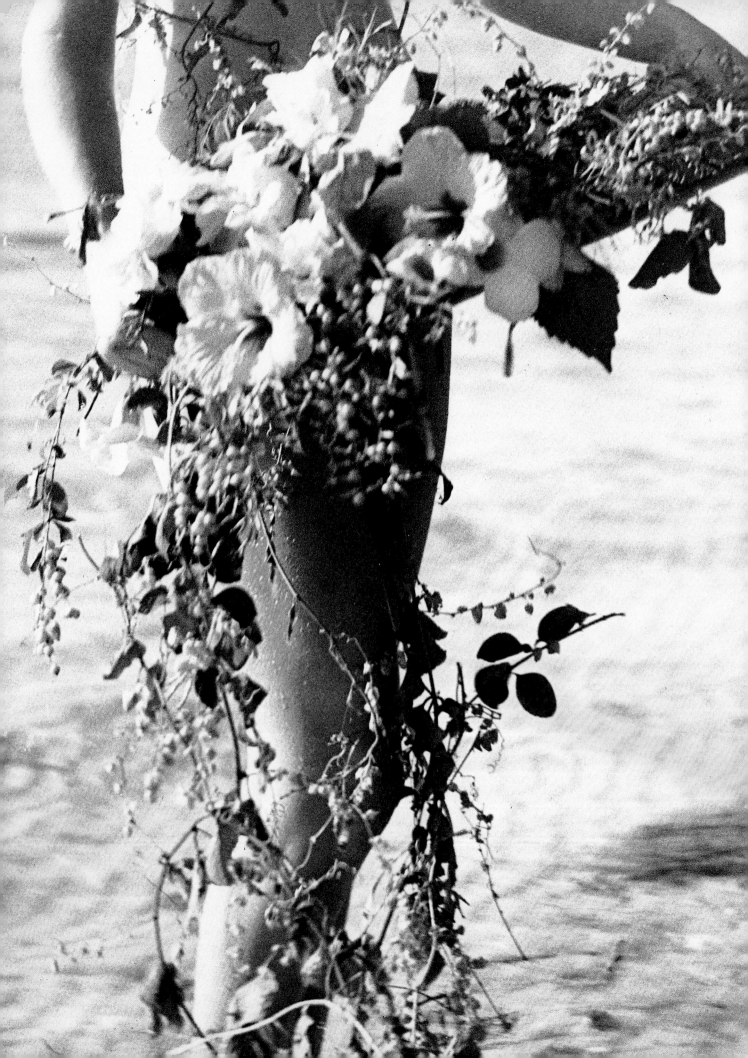

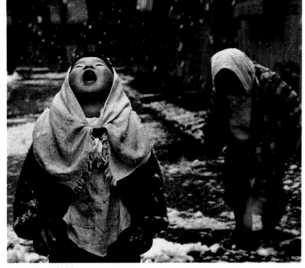

Japan. Unosuke Gamou

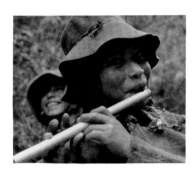

*O wonderful,*

*wonderful,*

*and most wonderful wonderful!*

*and yet again wonderful . . .*

William Shakespeare

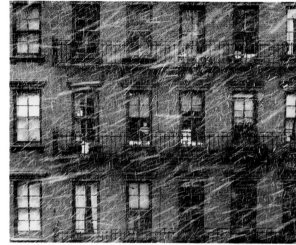

U.S.A. Paul Himmel

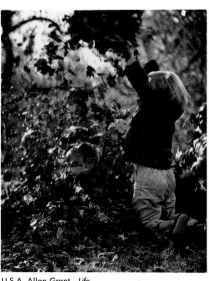

U.S.A. Allan Grant  *Life*

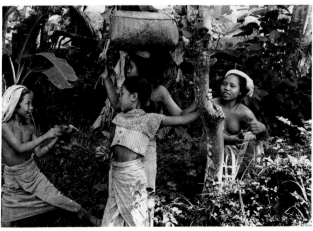

Java. Henri Cartier-Bresson  *Magnum*

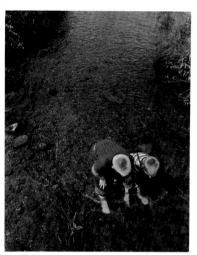

U.S.A. Jerry Cooke   YMCA

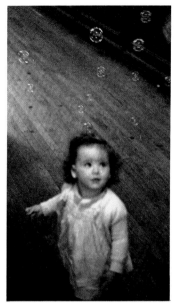

U.S.A. Homer Page

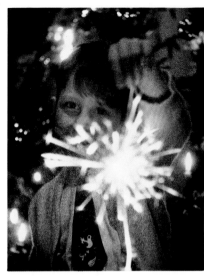

Switzerland. Sabine Weiss   *Rapho Guillumette*

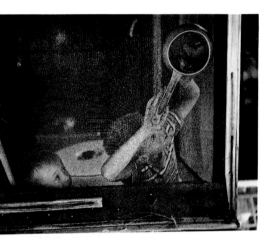

U.S.A. Don Ornitz

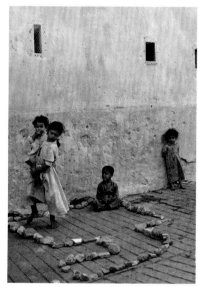

Tangiers. Charles Leirens

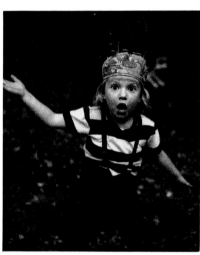

U.S.A. Suzanne Szasz

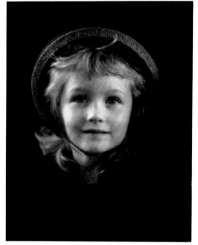

U.S.A. Barney Cowherd   *Louisville Courier-Journal & Times*

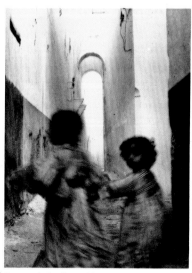

Morocco. Irving Penn   *Vogue*

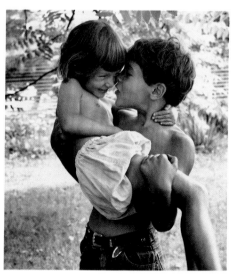

U.S.A. Richard Avedon   *Harper's Bazaar*

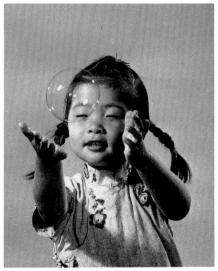

U.S.A. Gjon Mili

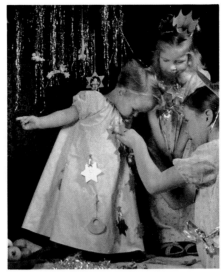

Germany. Annelise Rosenberg

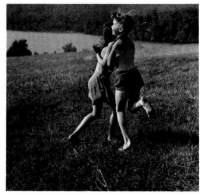

U.S.A. Barbara Morgan

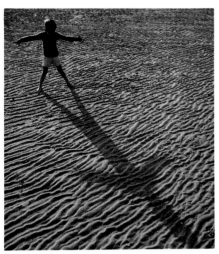

U.S.A. Toni Frissell

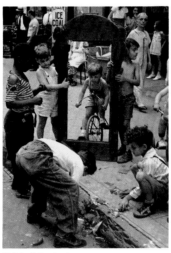

U.S.A. Helen Levitt

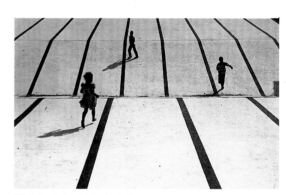

U.S.A. Sanford Roth   *Rapho Guillumette*

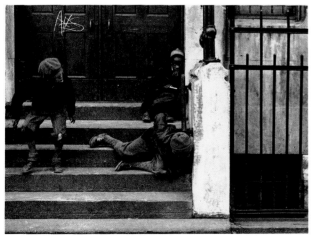

U.S.A. Helen Levitt

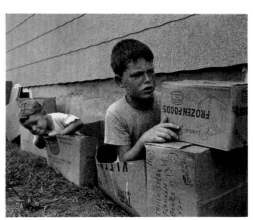

U.S.A. Guy Gillette   *Brackman Assoc.*

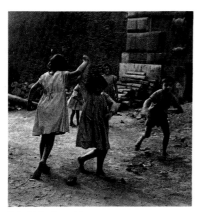

Italy. Hella Hammid

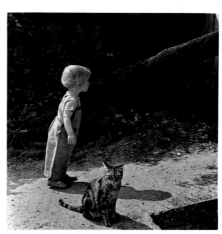

England. Lee Miller

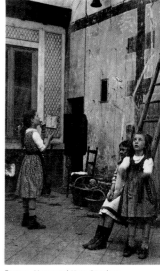

France. Mary and Kate Steichen
*Edward Steichen*

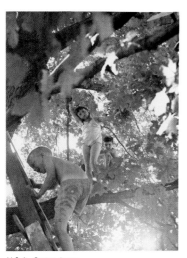

U.S.A. Carter Jones

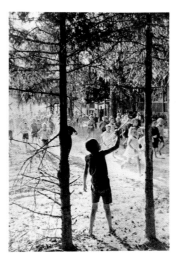

U.S.S.R. *Sovfoto*

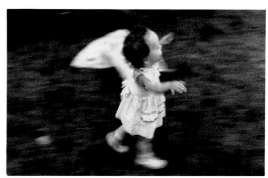

U.S.A. Edward Wallowitch

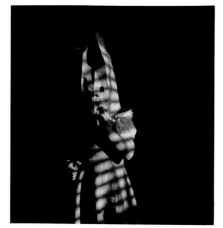

U.S.A. Harry Callahan

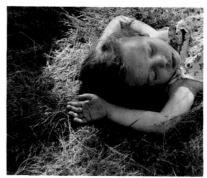

U.S.A. Gita Lenz

190

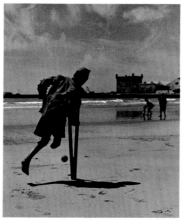

Morocco. Charles Trieschmann

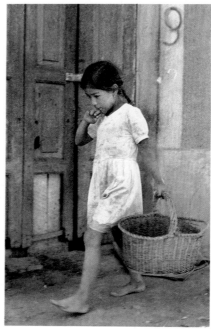

Mexico. Jasper Wood

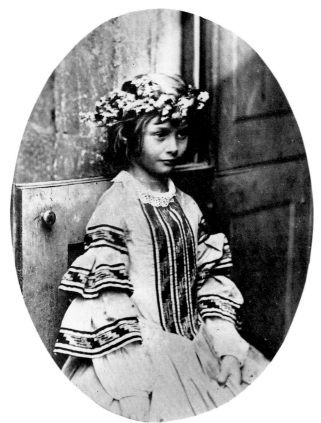

England. Lewis Carroll  *Circa 1862*

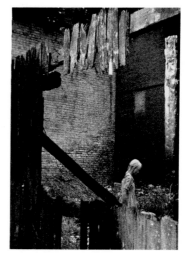

U.S.A. Farrell Grehan  *Popular Photography*

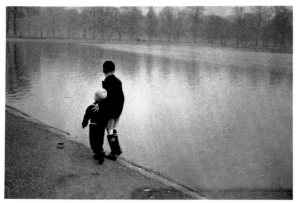

England. Ruth Orkin  *Popular Photography*

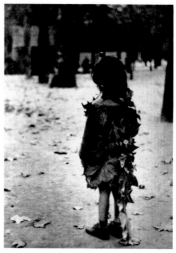

France. Edouard Boubat

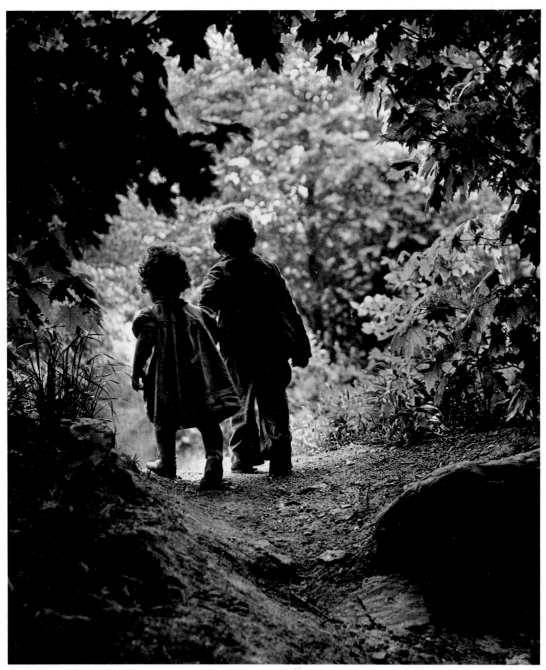

U.S.A. W. Eugene Smith

*A world to be born under your footsteps . . .*

St.-John Perse